The Way of Discovery

THE WAY
OF
DISCOVERY

An Introduction
to the Thought of
Michael Polanyi

Richard Gelwick

Oxford

NEW YORK   *University*   MCMLXXVII

Press

Permission to quote from Michael Polanyi, *Personal Knowledge: Towards a Post-Critical Philosophy*, published 1958 by the University of Chicago Press, Chicago, Illinois 60637 and Routledge and Kegan, Ltd., London, E. C. 4, England © copyright 1958 by Michael Polanyi, granted by the University of Chicago Press and by Routledge and Kegan Paul, Ltd.

Photographs appearing on pages 3, 29, 55, 83, 111, and 137 © Copyright 1977 by Arthur Tress. Reproduced by permission of the photographer.

Library of Congress Cataloging in Publication Data

Gelwick, Richard, 1931-
   The way of discovery.

   Bibliography: p.
   Includes index.
   1. Polanyi, Michael, 1891-   I. Title.
B945.P584G44   191   76-47429
ISBN 0-19-502192-4
ISBN 0-19-502193-2 pbk.

To Beverly, Jennifer, and Allen

ACKNOWLEDGMENTS

In my "focal awareness," to use Michael Polanyi's term, this book began with my meeting him in Berkeley in February 1962. In my "subsidiary awareness," to continue with Polanyi's usage, it began long ago with the problems, questions, and challenges posed by my mentors—civic and individual. My debts are beyond my thanking, but I wish to acknowledge some of them.

My relationship to Professor Michael Polanyi and his wife, Magda Polanyi, has been personal as well as professional since I began my study with him in 1962. A perfect book might express my appreciation for their kindness, generosity, and encouragement over the years. As any author knows too well, his book is not perfect, and I must express regret and take full responsibility for any failures of this work to live up to the advantages afforded me by their friendship.

Viewed chronologically, I also know in a "focal" way of the help of the late H. Richard Niebuhr of Yale, Charles McCoy and Durwood Foster in Berkeley, and of my associations with the Society of Explorers, now called the Polanyi Society.

The creative art of my former student, Christa Fuller Burns, contributes directly to Chapter III. The skills and patience of my secretary, Bedonna Clark, have helped in many ways in the completion of the manuscript.

To those who know Polanyi as a friend and daily household topic of conversation—my wife, Beverly, and my children, Jennifer and Allen—I give special thanks for their love and care.

Grants and fellowships from the Danforth Foundation, the Fund for Theological Education, and the Society for Religion in Higher Education have aided in various stages of my work. A sabbatical leave and the support of my colleagues at Stephens College encouraged the writing of the book. The careful assistance of Linda McBride and the editorial work of Vicky Bijur and the OUP staff were especially salutary.

R. G.

Columbia, Missouri
March, 1977

Contents

Introduction *xi*

i.
The Importance of Discovery

KNOWING AND BEING *3*

A GRASP OF OUR HISTORY *4*

A DYNAMO-COUPLING *6*

A CENTRAL DOGMA *14*

THE EXAMPLE OF SCIENTIFIC DISCOVERY *24*

ii.
From Scientist to Philosopher

THE ONLY GENUINE INTEREST *29*

INDUCTION INTO SCIENCE *31*

THE FREEDOM OF SCIENCE *35*

THE INAUGURAL ADDRESS *42*

TOWARDS A POST-CRITICAL PHILOSOPHY *47*

CONTENTS

iii.
A New Paradigm
A BASIC CHANGE 55
A NEW VIEW OF KNOWING 57
THE CLUE FROM GESTALT PSYCHOLOGY 61
NEW TERMS 65
TACIT KNOWING AND CLASSIC PHILOSOPHY 78
TACIT KNOWING AND PHILOSOPHY OF SCIENCE 79

iv.
A Heuristic Philosophy
THE POINT OF VIEW 83
SCIENCE AND REALITY 85
FOUNDATIONS OF TACIT KNOWING 91
THE PANORAMA OF TACIT KNOWING 94

v.
Invitation to Explorers
EXPLORATIONS IN THE MAKING 111
TRADITIONAL PHILOSOPHY 112
ANALYTICAL PHILOSOPHY 115
EXISTENTIALISM 118
PHILOSOPHY OF NATURAL AND SOCIAL SCIENCE 120
ART AND THEOLOGY 129
A FOCAL POINT FOR CHANGE 136

vi.
The Transformation of Imagination
HISTORY AND HOPE 137
AN END TO DICHOTOMIES 141
THE MEANING OF HUMANITY 149

Notes 159
Bibliography 175
Index 177

Introduction

A TIME FOR EXPLORERS

"It is the image of humanity immersed in potential thought that I find revealing for the problems of our day," writes Michael Polanyi. "It rids us of the absurdity of absolute self-determination, yet offers each of us the chance of creative originality, within the fragmentary area which circumscribes our calling. It provides us with the metaphysical grounds and organizing principle of a Society of Explorers."[1] Perhaps no other phrase so aptly encompasses the importance of Polanyi's investigations as "a Society of Explorers." It suggests both the centrality of discovery and the comprehensive significance of his philosophy. It pictures the intense effort of the individual pioneer who makes the great breakthrough. But it also images the social roots and ties that surround the seemingly individual triumph.

From his concentration upon the way of discovery in science, Polanyi has moved to universal conceptions that pertain to the most basic issues of our time. Polanyi's own life is an illustration of this duality of discovery and universality. At first, he was mainly a physical chemist speaking about the nature of scientific practice, but he soon found the philosophical issues of his laboratory bearing upon the broadest and deepest questions of existence in the twentieth century. To bring his mature philosophy with its foundation in the nature of scientific discovery into adequate perspective, it has to be set in a large field of problems and concerns.

Everyone admires discovery, yet few have studied it, and almost no one has seen in it the organizing point for a whole view of the world. Such a view is developed by Polanyi. Hence, thought on this scale warns and demands at the outset that we be prepared to look farther than usual, beyond the much described joy of creative endeavor, to the global problems of war, political strife, and loss of faith, to the scientific and metaphysical views of reality that underlie our civic, educational, economic, and religious institutions. If Polanyi's discovery of discovery is to be understood as he sees it, it is a calling to a new way of thinking for our whole society. It is the posting of a new frontier in thought, a new image of humanity, of an avant-garde that calls its company to see themselves as part of a grand and daring exploration in the cosmos. Before turning fully to this philosophy, it is important then to set out four assumptions that will indicate its general relevance.

First and foremost is the assumption that we are living in a crisis of civilized culture. It is a crisis that has been developing for at least several centuries and probably one that recurs periodically in every major cultural epoch as each civilization has to decide to renew itself and live or to decay and die. It is a crisis of the unifying beliefs and traditions that tie a society together and guide its functional progress. Once civilization and culture were virtually synonymous as we thought anthropologically of the artifical secondary environment that humans impose upon nature.[2] Then we saw the relative cultural values of the various civilizations but felt secure enough to assume that our civilization would continue in some form. Now we are going beyond the fear of value judgments and beyond the recognition that all cultures are relative and are stating plainly that we see before us the threats to the civil—the peaceful, orderly, and moral—conduct of global life. This condition is one that needs no extensive argument. The signs of it are rife. Dostoevsky prophesied in the last century that when God or the center of value died in our culture, all things would be permissible. In our century we have seen and are seeing his prophecy fulfilled. Our problem is to understand this crisis in a sufficiently inclusive yet essential way to do something responsible about it. Polanyi has found a crucial connection between our way of discovery in science and the central values of our society that suggests an alternative to the anomie growing throughout our world.

It should be added that the crisis of culture is not only a crisis of Western civilization, as many authors tend to emphasize. We have become globally bound together by the culture of modern science and technology. While there are older and distinctive cultures subsisting, the aspirations and policies of people and governments throughout the world are tied to the new culture of science (Chapter I).

A second assumption arises out of the nature of our cultural crisis, namely, the need for a basis of belief upon which we can act. We are in a crisis of belief about belief. Belief itself is discredited by the philosophies and outlooks that guide our present affairs. The impacts of ethical relativism and of scientific materialism have led to doubting any convictions that cannot be readily proved. There is a widespread lack of self-confidence in countering the eroding trends of nihilism. Uncertainty besets the believer in truth and good as ideals for moral conduct because they are lofty, vague, and difficult to define. Against the more obvious evidence of relativism and laboratory tests, the burden of proof appears unbearable. Truth, good, beauty, justice, courage, and honor are vague and value-laden terms. To try to cling to such ideals in the face of more tangible arguments is nearly impossible. Yet our capacity to hold on to ideals that are transcendent and hard to define is essential for the task at hand. Psychologically, our efforts are weakened when the cause seems futile. When the major symbols of meaning today tell us that we are fated to absurdity, we do not attempt to change the situation. At best, we try to live heroically while the world collapses around us, and devoid of any care for the future.[3] We need to know if there is a rational and credible basis upon which we can believe in ideals and goals that are less tangible and incapable of conclusive proof. While the tide appears to be against all values that require belief and commitment, there is a need for an under-girding of belief itself. As religion embodies and transmits the central values of a culture, this problem is also a religious issue. Moving from the beliefs necessary for the transmission of science and the training of scientists to the confident and passionate work of the creative scientist, Polanyi has seen a new foundation for the role of belief, a fiduciary character essential to all discovery.

In this connection, it is important to point out that this crisis of belief about belief is not limited to Western religions. We have, since the nineteenth century, acknowledged the high ethical quali-ties of the great religions of the world along with their unique differences. The influence of all these religions is now under attack and will increasingly be so as the non-Western nations increase their industrialization based upon scientific technology, unless an alternative understanding of belief and knowledge becomes con-vincing and viable.[4]

The third assumption is that there is a need for grounds for hope that are consonant with a scientific and rational understanding of the world. Generally, modern science has given us the best under-standing of the operation and potentialities of nature. The technol-ogy built upon this foundation, while dangerous today, is not inherently so if we have the will and wisdom to use it properly. What is needed is not a revolt against science, technology, or rationality but a new vision of science in which human life and its bond with nature can give us a creative home. Since the world views built upon science are largely responsible for our self-alienation and loss of confidence, it is acutely important that we have a picture in which we can be at one with both a scientific understanding of reality and the highest aspirations and beliefs of humanity. Know-ing what we do know through science, we need to understand how to maintain and increase our human greatness in a world studied and cultivated by scientific knowledge. For this reason, Polanyi's esteem and experience in science are especially important. He speaks from science and for science and opens up thereby a harmony between the "hard" sciences and the rest of our knowledge. The fourth assumption is partly opinion and partly fact. It seems that there is already under way a new movement against the denigration of values and humanity and for a belief in their potentialities. Despite the prevalence of apathy and resignation, despite the absence of widely-shared beliefs, and in the face of overwhelming pressures, there are many who are contending for the creative and humane possibilities of our lives. This book aims to aid and to encourage such persons by informing them of allies and in particular, of a major intellectual resource in their struggle. When the history of great ideas is done, it usually appears that what at first glimpse looked revolutionary is found upon later investigation to have been prepared and assisted by surrounding forces and events. At least, what is offered here is a view that is already being sought and approached by others. As always, some of the changes are at the fringe, sometimes negative. Nevertheless, it seems that there is abroad a variety of movements and of significant work by major thinkers (Chapters V and VI) that indicates a field of force pointing to a new paradigm (Chapter III).

A HEURISTIC PHILOSOPHY

From the perspective of these assumptions, the philosophy of Michael Polanyi is set forth. It is not because his work has suddenly become recognized widely that a book is needed about his thought. It is because his work itself is at first difficult and demanding.[5] Truly original and innovative thought could not be otherwise. Yet its relevance to our problems should not be curtailed. This philosophy undertakes the most thorough and profound analysis of all the main epistemological issues raised by science and produces an alternative proposal. No other thinker since the Second World War has produced such a comprehensive study of the epistemological questions. It is on the merits of its precision in its analysis of our problems, its focus upon the deepest issues of our life, and the range of its theory that Polanyi's thought deserves our consideration.

The philosophy of Polanyi is inherently controversial since it advocates a change from presently accepted modes of thought. It has been called "obscurantist" by competent philosophers.[6] It has also been praised as the work of "one of the greatest scientist-philosophers of our century."[7] One prominent contemporary philosopher has refused to take Polanyi seriously because Polanyi is difficult and Polanyi's approach does not fit into "academic philosophy."[8] Such varied reactions indicate the need for Polanyi's philosophy to be offered in a larger forum of discussion where the awareness of the grave problems of our age facilitates a hearing. As we shall see (Chapter IV), Polanyi's thought calls for a major reorientation of our knowledge, and the criticisms offered have to be weighed fairly against Polanyi's grasp of our situation.

The presentation of Polanyi's philosophy is in itself a major task. Since it is independent of any single philosophical school and arose from his own reflections, this philosophy has to be approached as distinctive and unique. The attempt to present it as a type of philosophy already known turns out to be Procrustean. To be sure, the philosophy has affinities and continuities with previous philosophies. Yet it is new and should not be prematurely classified. As in the case of other original philosophies such as those of Kierkegaard and Whitehead, it may be best to take a term from the philosophy itself to designate it. I am proposing here, for reasons that will become apparent, to refer to it as "heuristic" philosophy, but the term has to be understood with the significance that Polanyi gives it. More important than the name is the new understanding of knowledge and of ourselves that Polanyi has achieved.

Another challenge in presenting Polanyi's thought is its breadth. Ostensibly, his philosophy is a theory of knowledge or epistemology. Although the work begins as an inquiry into knowledge, it soon expands into the widest dimensions of that subject and becomes also a philosophy bearing upon ontology and ethics. To put it another way, Polanyi's thought is highly interdisciplinary, drawing upon data from nearly every major department of knowledge. Political theorists, sociologists, economists, psychologists, historians, artists, and educators, as well as lawyers, theologians, philosophers, engineers, and scientists, have found large areas of his work relevant to their special tasks. Hence, the usual philosophical discussion of a topic as theory of knowledge or ethics will not suffice. One needs to employ these philosophical tools and be prepared to expand quickly the framework of the discussion beyond the usual philosophical categories.

OBJECTIVE IDEAL, OBJECTIVISM, AND OBJECTIVITY

One of the most important, yet often misunderstood, issues in Polanyi's thought is his proposal of an alternative to the ideal of objective scientific knowledge. Polanyi deeply believes in objectivity but of a different kind and on a different basis from what is widely understood.[9] For Polanyi there is a false objectivity that has taken over the modern mind and become expressed in what is called "the scientific outlook." He describes this scientific outlook well when he says, "The declared aim of modern science is to establish a strictly detached, objective knowledge."[10] He also clarifies what he means by this false type of objectivity when he states the aim of his thought: "I start by rejecting the ideal of scientific detachment. In the exact sciences, this false ideal is perhaps harmless, for it is in fact disregarded there by scientists. But we shall see that it exercises a destructive influence in biology, psychology and sociology and falsifies our whole outlook far beyond the domain of science."[11] To keep Polanyi's target of this false type of objectivity clear, I shall refer to it usually as "the objective ideal of knowledge," "objectivism," or "the scientific outlook" in contrast with his belief in a genuine objectivity and in a truer description of scientific discovery.

The choice of the terms "the objective ideal of knowledge" and "objectivism" is justified on several grounds. First, Polanyi's attack is upon an outlook that is older and wider than positivism, as we shall see. Positivism is an outgrowth of a deeper epistemological error in the rise of modern science. Second, this false objectivity is a paradigm that operates as a central dogma in our society. In this sense it is a distorted ideal toward which humans strive. Once this false objectivity is understood, we can turn to that truer objectivity, seen by Polanyi in the example of scientific discovery, as it personally participates in that reality that beckons and guides us to ever broadening and surprising horizons of understanding.

After more than ten years of introducing his thought in teaching and articles, I am convinced that the best way for most people to enter into his philosophy is to follow the story of his own intellectual development. People frequently ask where to begin in understanding Polanyi's thought, expecting me to recommend one of his books. But I find that the best place to begin is where Polanyi began, with the problems and disasters of our century and with the way in which they call for a fresh examination of the grounds of knowledge (Chapter I). Once the problems and the questions are set, we can follow Polanyi toward his new view (Chapters III and IV).

This approach is admittedly a sympathetic one, bent upon calling attention to what may be the first general articulation of a new model of human understanding for our civilization. The attempt to convey the totality of his thought, without the degree of complexity that Polanyi himself presents, suffers the danger of oversimplification. The novelty of Polanyi does consist of his appreciation of much thought that has gone before, as well as his wider grasp of its implications and reorganization of it into a wholly new and constructive view. Many other scholars are now engaged in this more technical and elaborate investigation of Polanyi's thought.[12] At this point, my aim is to set forth the wider range of his thought. I am convinced of its importance and share his belief that all humans are called to be a part of a "Society of Explorers."[13] It is to be hoped that Polanyi's sense of adventure and wonder will come through to those who read this book, and that his effort to follow knowledge from the point of view of discovery will provide substantial foundations for a more human future.

The Way of Discovery

i. The Importance of Discovery

KNOWING AND BEING

Thinkers in the last several generations have had to work in the midst of the most terrible of human possibilities, the growing sense of an irrational and absurd universe. The words of John Donne on the threshold of the scientific revolution, "Tis all in pieces, all coherence gone . . . ," have rung true. After three centuries of scientific progress, expansive hopes, and enlightened humanitarian reforms much of our world view has lost its coherence and its adequacy. We live in an "unsponsored" universe. Beset by this collapse of ultimate and unifying beliefs and foundations, thought is adrift in a vast cosmos without distinct origins or directions.

The movement from the early confidence of the scientific revolution to the existential despair of the twentieth century has left us with a bewildering view of knowing and being. In an absurdist world view, the question becomes "Why create or learn at all?" Creativity and intelligent activity seem to be only epiphenomenal defiances of the ultimate absurdity of life. Yet creativity has flourished in art and science. Humans have extended their senses and imagination in ways never experienced before. Reality that was once so clear has become ambiguous and uncertain, but we have been learning to live with ambiguity. Humans in the crisis of meaning have found that they can structure their experience. Whether or not this structuring is well-founded is a part of the puzzle. Do we really make ourselves? Have we once again confronted in our extremity the opportunity for a fresh understanding of our metaphysical roots? At this level, Polanyi's philosophy begins.

A GRASP OF OUR HISTORY

The seminal clue to our modern predicament came to Michael Polanyi from the nature of scientific discovery, but the problems that propelled him to this clue were the violent and brutal events of our century. He began with an awareness that our century is not just another case in history of the cruelties of the struggles for power, but that it is the most destructive century, not even counting the lethal power of nuclear weapons, of any century in the modern era.[1] This devastation has to be seen against the hopes of three centuries in which Western civilization saw itself as progressing toward humanitarian and liberal institutions under the guidance of reason based on science.

Born March 11, 1891, in Budapest, Polanyi in his lifetime has witnessed both the unity and the dissolution of European culture. He remembers "an almost forgotten past of peace, of bold intellectual and artistic enterprise and of continuous progress towards liberal ideals."[2] He recalls the greatness of European centers of thought and compares what they were with what they are today. In thinking of this contrast and the magnitude and the madness of the killing of more than fifty million persons since 1914, he seeks an answer to the question of how the most morally motivated and the most liberally inquiring period in history could culminate in such destruction.

To Polanyi, the scale of violence and catastrophe is not accounted for by pointing to the art of modern warfare or to the growth of world population. He recognizes that the toll of the Thirty Years' War or the Black Death of the fourteenth century is proportionately greater in number than our current devastation. But the difference today is that the foundations of our culture have been nearly destroyed, while the previous disasters only ravaged and impoverished the population. Belief in and pursuit of the goals of their culture continued. In our century, we are confronted with unparalleled harm and with the loss of faith in moral and humane goals that can be pursued by persons as responsible agents. In more traditional terms, we have lost the grounds of man's and woman's spiritual existence.

Grasping our dangerous situation is itself a problem. Few have a historical perspective from which to see the crisis at which we have arrived. Furthermore, our tools for analysis are enmeshed in an outlook that cannot fully appreciate or entertain the larger issues that shape our destiny. Polanyi tells a story of an address to the Medical Section of the British Psychological Society in which he spoke on the modern mind.[3] The chairman expressed disappointment, saying that he had hoped for something more substantial. Polanyi commented that given the chairman's point of view, this was right. Polanyi was speaking of the modern mind as a body of ideas having their origin in thought, whereas in the chairman's profession it was customary to regard ideas as the rationalization of drives, of guilt feelings or anxiety, or aggression, or insecurity. Granting the importance of the tangible forces of infantile traumas, broken homes, and industrialization, Polanyi sees such analysis as failing to cope with the greater question of the presuppositions that shape our period. The preference for dealing with what is most tangible and material causes many to ignore the influence of ideas on our history.

Ideas have played a decisive and controlling role in our cultural crisis. Polanyi states that "the main influence of science on modern man has not been through the advancement of technology, but through the effect of science on our world view."[4] "It was not technology that produced the ideologies which brought the disasters of the Twentieth Century, nor the feeling of absurdity and contempt for human society that is current today."[5] What we have to deal with is "the scientific image of the world" developed by the modern mind.

The import of this view for all those who focus upon the future and technology should not be missed. Polanyi is asserting that the most fundamental problem is the outlook that guides our imagination and concern, not technology itself. To begin an assault upon our problems, we need first to have a grasp of these underlying ideas that fostered the epic cataclysms of our time. It will be found that not only did these ideas generate destruction, but they also falsified the foundations of knowledge itself. The reorientation of knowing will be found in the nature of discovery.

A DYNAMO-COUPLING

When Polanyi looks at the history of the modern period, there are two salient facts that hold his attention. One is the creative development of natural science, and the other is the drive for social and moral progress. These two aspects are both the wonder and the bewilderment of the period. The growth of the natural sciences and the achievements based upon them is one of the most admirable and remarkable events in all of human history. While the world strode forward in its understanding of nature's laws, it also set forth on a mission to liberate and to dignify the status of all human life by the same rationality that was guiding science.

These twins of science and social reform, born of a new outlook, promising in their adolescence, surprisingly became in their adult years enemies of their own family and heritage. Scientific technology, once the unquestioned guardian and builder of a better world, became a weapon of destruction. Social and political philosophies based upon science became absolute and tyrannical ideologies.

Given the potential of modern science and its humanitarian vision, Polanyi sees a compelling need to understand the tragedies that it produced. These two facts of modern history provide definition and focus for understanding the modern mind. The combination of scientific progress and of humanitarian reform ending in an age of violence poses a problem. What is the mechanism of interaction that brought violence out of these distinctively worthy movements? What latent flaw was hidden from view in their origin and development? What condition released their destructive character?

The data for Polanyi's consideration of these questions, as we shall see in the next chapter, came to a great extent from his experience of two world wars and the Russian Communist Revolution. The Nazi and the Stalinist regimes, though vastly different in their specific political beliefs, manifested the two features that were supposed to serve the general welfare of the state. Both proclaimed programs based upon scientific theories. Both justified terrible atrocities on the grounds that such actions were necessary for the moral aims of their parties. After the fact, it is easier to judge the scientific merits of these claims and their moral integrity. Such easy evaluations are cheap and unilluminating. They do not produce sufficient understanding to avoid future repetitions. After the reprehensible becomes apparent, it is simple to be against wrong. The deeper question remains of how major ideals of our culture could turn from apparent blessings into lethal effects.[6]

Upon examination, Polanyi found that given the right cultural attitudes, the two bright developments of the modern period did combine to form a passionate, ruthless, and intolerant social force. He called this phenomenon a "dynamo-objective coupling."[7] The fusion of scientific objectivism with intense moral passions produces a relentless drive for social amelioration that brooks no dissent or opposition. Convinced of its own righteousness, this coupling is also blind to its own weaknesses and errors. Joined in this peculiar way, two good features of our culture produced

[7]

"moral inversion."[8] Morality, instead of guiding us to worthy goals, became the dynamo to force a supposedly scientific view upon others. This scientifically-determined view repelled all criticism because of the assumed certainty of its truth. Though motivated by moral passions, the urged position was immune to moral criticism.

To understand the nature of this development, Polanyi observes how the story begins, long before the twentieth-century wars and revolutions, in the waning foundations of European culture. For a society to have independence of thought and a love of truth and intellectual values, it has to be supported by tacit cultural assumptions that uphold these pursuits. The capacity of individuals to pursue the truth and to share it grows from a community that accepts the obligation to seek and to submit to the truth. Such a conviction is a shared one that forms a part of the individual's upbringing. But this tradition of the pursuit of the truth is liable to doubt. Upon examination, it will be found that our commitment to the truth is culturally formed and appears external and arbitrary. A disturbance through such doubt arose when the objective ideal of knowledge began to take hold of the modern mind.[9] Knowledge that appeared to be founded on tradition and personal involvement was classed as subjective and insubstantial. The outcome was to upset belief in the power of thought to pursue truth through free inquiry and discussion. The objective standard led to a belief in the material and the impersonal criteria of true knowledge. By the time totalitarian ideologies appeared, the standard of truth for many had already become that which could be objectively demonstrated.

The transformations of our mental outlook by the growth of the objective ideal of knowledge were more far-reaching than any political ideology itself. This outlook creates instability in minds and in civic institutions, leading to nihilistic beliefs and actions. We could speak of the objective ideal of knowledge as a sickness because it denies the healthy or normal functions of the individual and society. The human person is, by his or her evolutionary inheritance, an explorer. Polanyi traces our articulate intelligence down the scale of life as far as worms and amoebae, finding in them a general alertness and an urge to achieve control over situations confronting them.[10] Here he finds a principle of the living organism actively participating in the shaping of its "knowledge" and accepting it as a token of reality. This principle continues in us through the enormous advantage of conceptual language stored and transmitted from generation to generation. But the objective ideal contradicts this principle twice. First, objectivism repudiates our valid contribution to what we know by trying to purge our participation in knowing. Second, objectivism tries to reject the framework of knowledge transmitted to us as our natural habitat through which we continue our explorations. Such attempts are not mere ideas but deformations of the structure of our own existence. Persistent efforts to deny our nature would be bound to produce pathological conditions.[11] The drive of our intellectual passions to make sense out of the situations facing them would have to find some outlet.

The modern world is filled with many responses to this development. Some are mainly intellectual self-deceptions, such as scientists' pretending to study living subjects without interest in such subjects' bearing upon human existence. Others are more destructive, promoting philosophies in which the individual tries to assimilate himself to the model of a machine. Most apparently destructive, with the obvious cost to human life, are political ideologies that invite the individual to surrender his or her self to an interpretation of all of life while telling the individual that this interpretation is objectively true and the individual bears no responsibility for it. This truth, he is assured, is independent of all personal beliefs.

The change to an objective ideal of knowledge involves a denial of intellectual values embodied in ritual, law, custom, art, and social lore. It allows for the advocacy of immediate revolutionary change. Instead of thought and life growing through the pursuit of permanent and transcendent aspirations intimated by past traditions, progress becomes the establishment of a utopia already conceived and waiting. The perennial tension between thought and society that produces change is eliminated. As the indepen-

[9]

dence of thought comes to an end, the self is prepared to accept an external answer. In short, these are the mental alterations preparatory to modern totalitarianism and other forms of moral inversion.

The understanding of the mechanism of the dynamo-objective coupling that produces moral inversion is crucial to diagnosing the difficulties of our time. Instead of rating our period as an immoral one, it points out that it is one of the most morally concerned in history. As Polanyi says, "Never in the history of mankind has the hunger for brotherhood and righteousness exercised such power over the minds of men as today."[12]

To cope with our problems, we need to recognize "the moral force of immorality," the way nihilistic acts satisfy moral motives. In turn, we are directed to our general theory of knowledge, the way our society conceives things to be true. For it is by the combination of the objective ideal of knowledge with the highest moral aspirations that we have incurred our modern disasters. The dynamo-objective coupling explains how our heritage of moral and humanitarian concern became the servant of ideologies and world views that treat persons as things.

The mechanism of the dynamo-objective coupling was suggested to Polanyi by Levy-Brühl's study of primitive mental operations.[13] Levy-Brühl observed how a personal feeling or motive was identified with an external event. He called this phenomenon "participation." An example of its operation is seen in the case of a villager's thinking that the death of a hunter by a lion is a manifestation of his fellow tribesman's envy. This phenomenon is also seen in the way that plagues and natural catastrophes are sometimes understood as the punishments from or evil intentions of supernatural beings. Again, it is the identification of feeling or motives with external events. Polanyi observed that this phenomenon is seen most recently in the way that historicism has replaced the will of God in history by an idea of Historic Necessity. Yet Historic Necessity is imputed to act with moral attributes, such as doing what is right or fitting. It is upon this mechanism of coupling feelings or motives with manifest external events that moral inversion develops.

[10]

Polanyi takes the case of Marxism under Lenin and Stalin as a chief example of moral inversion arising from the dynamo-objective coupling. Marxism thrived and grew rapidly because it appealed to the twin ideals of the modern period, humanitarianism and scientific objectivism. From the time of the French Revolution, the moral demands for liberty, equality, and fraternity spread all over the globe to millions of persons who had previously accepted exploitation and squalor.[14] Marxism offered a program that promised fulfillment of these demands for justice, and it made the offer with the authority of a scientific interpretation of history. These facts illuminate the rapid growth of Marxism and its appeal to intellectuals.

Marxism couples moral motives with its economic interpretation of history. The sinister side of Marxism developed from the peculiar way its theory both contradicted and utilized moral motives. Looking at capitalist society, Marxism identified morality with the bourgeois interests that maintained a class structure. It advocated overthrow of the capitalist society so that wealth could flow to all. This attack was proclaimed in economic terms, not in the slogans of liberty and freedom, for such moral terms were viewed as the sentiments of the middle-class capitalists who did not promote material realities for all. Marxism renounced morality as espoused in traditional terms, yet reaped its support by claiming to offer in economic terms what was desired by all persons as their right.

This type of Marxism under Lenin and Stalin produced fanaticism. It denied any intrinsic force to morality itself by saying that moral ideals were used by the bourgeoisie to exploit the proletariat. It even denied its own moral aspirations by saying that they were inevitable developments of scientific principles of history. Yet, these scientific assertions were accepted partly because of the moral satisfaction they offered. The moral passions of Marxism were decked out in scientific dress. Open moral objection to Stalinist purges or to unjust imprisonment could be brushed aside as unscientific. Hence, Marxism became an example of the moral force of immorality.

[11]

The case of Nazi fascism also illustrates moral inversion arising from the dynamo-objective coupling phenomenon.[15] Hitler's movement was rooted in a belief in German Romantic nihilism, a doctrine which taught the right of a superior individual to impose his will upon the rest of the world and the right of a nation to fulfill its destiny regardless of moral trespasses. Even though the persecution and the aggression were evil, they were upheld as proper instruments for the unquestionable aims of the Nazi state. Thus, we have the enthusiasm of the German Youth movement's accepting immoral actions as their true duty.

The examples of totalitarian ideologies, while telling, are only an aspect of the larger predicament of our time. We are faced with living with two immensely valuable convictions—the value of human growth and development and the scientific understanding of nature—that tend to form a threat to our existence. Our belief in the value and potential of human persons and society is a belief of inexhaustible range. To hold such a belief is to live always with the possibility of further development. If we ever demand or expect complete realization of this ideal, we experience frustration and disappointment. It is at this point that our belief in the objectivist scientific approach to nature comes to jeopardize our life. By being understood as a method that makes all truth explicit and detached from those who uphold it, this view has both activated our moral urgency and deprived us of guidelines for channeling our concern.

The sense of scientific objectivism has led to a revulsion at our hypocrisy in not living up to our moral ideals. This desire to honestly expose our faults demands immediate recognition of failures and changes to the right behavior. Here the radical attempt to establish the moral perfection intrinsic in our hopes for human society inevitably encounters its own finitude and inadequacies. But this radical protest and quest for improvement are unable to control and to stabilize themselves. In the very nature of its scientific beliefs, society has undermined the moral restraints that should question and nurture its life. In the demand for objectivism, it has created pervasive self-doubt. To cling to our humanitarian visions, we have to believe in the value and power of ideals that are traditional and transcendent. These are values we know but cannot fully define or objectify. Truth, beauty, justice, love, and honor are such ideals. The notion of the objective ideal reduces them to petty and pedestrian proportions. Beauty and love become emotions. Justice and honor become conformity to current conceptions. Truth becomes the mathematical measurement of quantities. In such a situation, the potentiality of genius is imprisoned, human creativity sterilized.

Still, no moral inversion can completely succeed.[16] Even fanatical regimes that deny moral authority make persuasive appeals betraying their concern for a sense of right. The Hungarian Revolution of 1956 bears witness to the persistence of thought, morality, art, justice, and religion as autonomous powers despite their widespread repudiation.[17] Subtler forms of moral inversion are also common among intellectuals who claim to be neutral and objective yet continue to act with passion for human values that their philosophies officially scorn. In this residual moral expression is potential for change.

Our civilization is in a strange plight. It has launched itself upon a grand mission only to find itself in self-doubt and disintegration. The goals that it has set itself are ones that continually demand change. Such a dynamic society is always adventuresome, promising new horizons and richness. In the process of seeking these goals, we have corrupted them with doubt about all goals that cannot be made fully articulate and realizable. In this loss of the credibility of our vision, we have been left to the powers of what seems most tangible. The variations with which this consequence has developed are many. In one form, it has led to the conclusion that there is no ultimate meaning except absurdity. In another, it has led to the exercise of exposing our failures, the partial joy of honest analysis without a commitment to suffer for any long-range ideals. In still other forms, it has led to a grim way of life determined by the conceptions of a machine.

Although we are presently beyond the nihilism that led millions into totalitarian ideologies, we are not beyond the instabilities of the modern outlook that produced that holocaust. Leading biolo-

[13]

gists such as Jacques Monod proclaim the absolute independence of objective knowledge as the way to truth and regard all ethics as subjective choice.[18] American democracy struggles to determine if there is a tradition of truth and honesty to be respected by all citizens or if law is but the convention and judgment of the powerful. Recurrent cycles of university student rebellion and apathy in Europe and America indicate a new nihilism of disgust with the hypocrisy of their elders and alienation from the general aims of society. Even so, we are still morally earnest despite our general theory of knowledge that questions the validity of transcendent human aims and values. We are also convinced of the virtue of the scientific approach. We are not likely to abandon these two convictions. In this situation, we need to find out how human values and scientific understanding can coexist without producing nihilistic consequences. Polanyi has pointed to the way in which skepticism, fostered by the objective ideal of knowledge from science, released the dynamic passions of Christian morality that led to our predicament. The next question concerns the background and nature of the objective ideal itself.

A CENTRAL DOGMA

C. P. Snow has spoken of "two cultures," describing the gap between science and the rest of our society. Polanyi has answered Snow by observing that in a deeper sense than Snow considered, we really have one culture, not two.[19] While there is a major disjunction between the knowledge of the general public and the technical knowledge of scientists, the authority of science exerts a comprehensive power over the minds of most persons today. Science exercises the kind of authoritative sway that Christian religion once did. To assert that a person, or his idea, is "unscientific" is the severest charge. It is in this way that we have to approach the objective ideal of knowledge. It is not an ideal directly and explicitly taught, so much as it is the central dogma of the scientific age. To speak of science is to speak of a vast domain. Polanyi distinguishes the content and the process of science from the scientific outlook or world view. It is not the laws of thermodynamics, quantum mechanics, or photosynthesis, but the objective ideal that has become dominant. People refer to this dogma in textbooks, but they usually do so as if it were self-evident. Furthermore, it is the foundation attitude for a variety of philosophical developments, including modern rationalism, empiricism, positivism, and reductionism. The understanding of the rise and power of this ideal involves an appreciation of both the modern scientific revolution and its philosophic expressions. It is in both the glamour of the scientific triumphs and in the philosophies that followed that we find the development of our frame of mind.

Events and ideas have combined to convince the modern world that the objective ideal of knowledge is the method of science and the hallmark of truth, even though it is not practiced in science nor capable of establishing truth.[20] The attractiveness of the objective ideal will turn out to be its pseudo-substitution of fact for responsible commitment, the appearance of holding knowledge without risk or values.

Polanyi sees the epitome of the objective ideal of knowledge in a formulation by Laplace.[21] Writing in the beginning of the nineteenth century, Laplace articulated the vision of how the methods of an impersonal science of measurement could provide universal knowledge. "He wrote that an intelligence which knew at one moment of time 'all the forces by which nature is animated and the respective positions of the entities which compose it . . . would embrace in the same formula the movements of the largest bodies in the universe and those of the lightest atom: nothing would be uncertain for it, and the future, like the past, would be present to its eyes.'"[22] This vision of knowledge reveals the standard that has developed from modern science. It pictures reality and the knowledge of it as being the calculation of the forces affecting matter. It is mechanical and atomic. Reality is made of particles that obey the laws of physics. In order to know the past or predict the future, we would only have to know the location, time, and velocity of all the atoms of the world. From these data, we could have complete knowledge. The extent to which this dream continues is seen in the popular beliefs today that computers can replace creative human intelligence and that the physics and chemistry of DNA can explain all levels of living beings.[23] It is the grounds of this attitude that Polanyi seeks to uncover and to change.

Polanyi finds that the elements of the objective ideal of knowledge are not new, but these ideas formed a persuasive alliance in the modern age.[24] The ingredients of the objective ideal go back to antiquity, but its present overpowering strength is the sequel of the Copernican revolution.

Three elements from antiquity that have come to form the modern scientific outlook are moral skepticism, mechanism, and moral perfectionism. Moral skepticism and mechanism are distinctively Greek. Greek Pyrrhonism was phenomenalist, teaching that we could not know the nature of things but only how they appear to our senses. As a consequence of this view, it was held that certain knowledge was impossible in moral matters and that we should take an attitude of resignation on questions of right and wrong.

The Greek atomists, represented by Democritus, held a mechanical view of reality. Democritus conceived of the whole world as nothing but the interactions of atoms, the most influential scientific view that we have received from the Greeks. The implication of Democritus' view was that the mechanical properties of things, their motion and their atomic shape, are their primary character, an idea later revived by Galileo and Locke. Beauty, honor, and truth are secondary qualities, mere conventions, values that we cannot know, if they even exist.

The third element from antiquity is Jewish and Christian. From this source comes a commitment to the moral perfection of every person and of society according to the attributes of an infinite God, a commitment that demands the pursuit of an inexhaustible righteousness. This goal of moral growth and development according to a belief in divine love and brotherhood implies a view of progress and change for all humanity. It is the basis of the social dynamism of Western civilization.

[16]

The first stage in the story of the way these three components from the past became the objective ideal of knowledge is the modern scientific revolution. Beginning with Copernicus, man was ousted from his central position in the universe and the theological cosmos was shaken. The heavenly sphere of divine perfection toward which medieval Christians strived was dissolved into a space without limits, without shape or center.

Yet the feat of Copernicus was inspired by the ancient Pythagorean tradition that relied upon the harmony of nature and of number rather than upon our senses as a guide to scientific knowledge. Copernicus's heliocentric system was based upon the elegance and beauty of its explanations of the movements of the planets rather than upon the accumulation of new empirical observations. The same Pythagorean quest for harmonious numbers and geometrical excellence continued in Kepler, who ecstatically expressed his astronomical work as rational thought communing with the divine order.

With Galileo, a transition to number as mere recording of events begins. Although Galileo remained Pythagorean with respect to the perfect order of the world, he articulated the ancient mechanist view that shape, size, quantity, and motion are the primary qualities that the scientist should seek to examine. Later, with Newton, the change begun by Galileo was established as normative when his general theory of gravitation seemed to bring all the matter in the universe under the rule of mechanical laws. The impact of Newton's success was to teach us to confine scientific investigation to those things that are capable of measurement and calculation. This view, too, was a theoretical one, using a space-time map of mass in motion to predict the behavior of material objects. But the nature of theory had changed from the Pythagorean tradition. Reason and experience were separated. Mathematics lost its inherent connection with nature and became a recording device of the contingent events of the world. The harmony of the world was gone. The world that remained was just whatever happened to be the case. The message of the scientific revolution was to place an emphasis upon mathematics and experiment divorced from our personal contribution in using them. The personal genius of the

[17]

pioneers of this major revolution was subsumed under the emerging idea of scientific method. The eclipse of the personal coefficient, especially in discovery, had begun.

The second part of the drama is the development of the critical attitude of the modern period exemplified in philosophy. The intellectual forces of the Renaissance and the Reformation, leavened by the new approach in science, quickened the spirit of criticism. It became a common assumption to this day that "the acceptance of unproven beliefs was the broad road to darkness, while truth was approached by the straight and narrow path of doubt."[25] We were warned against the unproven beliefs instilled in us since childhood. Religious dogma, the authority of the ancients, the teaching of the schools, the maxims of the nursery were all seen as a body of tradition imposed upon us by others.

Spurred by this critical outlook, philosophers began to try to wipe away all dubitable knowledge and to establish only what was certain. Descartes set forth universal doubt as the method to eliminate opinions and illusions and to found knowledge upon what was rationally clear and indubitable. While Descartes stressed the mathematical side of the new science, John Locke stressed its empirical dimension. He expressed what has become a common sense view of science today, namely, that true knowledge is based upon the evidence of the senses.

The contribution of Polanyi is not in his recounting and systematizing the philosophers of this period but in his recognizing the chain of influence through the central figures of this period that demolished our reliance upon tradition and impersonalized our ideal of knowledge. "The method of doubt is the logical corollary of objectivism."[26] It teaches that if we give up all voluntary components of belief, there will be left behind the residue of objective evidence.

The search for certainty free from the fetters of the past or personal bias established modern skepticism in the long run. The rationalist approach of Descartes and Kant not only succeeded in purifying the mind but resulted, paradoxically, in leaving the physical world as the most certain. The empiricists, following Locke and Hume, were compelled to admit the uncertainty of even their knowledge of the world and their sense experience, so probable knowledge was the best that could be offered. The implications of these developments were yet to be realized in the centuries that followed.

The first phase of the working out of the meaning of the critical philosophy was the period known as the Enlightenment. It is at this point that the moral perfectionism of the Jewish and Christian tradition became secularized into the aims of the modern age. In three ways the Enlightenment consolidated the achievements of the seventeenth-century scientific revolution into a new world view. First, it formulated the methods of science in terms that made science seem to be the surest way to truth. Second, it replaced the conflict of faith and doubt by making reason, as understood by the new science, the arbiter of conflict. Third, it adopted the program of humanizing the world by the application of the principles of scientific rationalism. The Enlightenment was an age in possession of a new confidence and fired by a new view of the world.

As a consequence of these new ideas of science and philosophy, major transformations took place. Paramount among these changes was the French Revolution, marking the dividing line between the static societies of the past and the dynamic societies of today. The noblest features of science were taken over to build a better world. Voltaire, Diderot, and Condorcet projected upon human affairs a vision of unlimited progress, a world where the free pursuit of individual happiness would lead to the concordant happiness of all. "This was the hour when we Western people started the enterprise that no man had undertaken before, to live by reason based on science."[27]

These changes were not a simple shedding of old views for new ones. They were revolutionary, and the new view in the long run would reveal its antecedents. At the outset, the Enlightenment ideals promised to give a moral and rational approach to problems. Instead they set in motion the moral passion in the guise of the objective ideal that would nearly consume us in the twentieth century. It is here that Polanyi's perception of the logic of this history is most penetrating. Doubt of beliefs, always a human

[19]

problem, had become intense through the critical philosophy. The religious clashes, the new sense of individual freedom, and the conflict of biblical views with the new science raised doubt to a breaking point. In this moment, the Enlightenment philosophies offered an alternative. Doubt could be eliminated by accepting what was rationally, that is, scientifically, certain. Morals, through such persons as Bentham, then became a science, the utilitarian calculation of the greatest happiness for the greatest number. Science itself became the process of calculation and measurement of matter. In this way, people were not asked to uphold beliefs that might be dubitable, and they were encouraged by the moral sense of their rationality. Everything, it seemed, had been brought under the clarity of the new science.

Underground another stream was still running. This current of contradiction between moral skepticism and moral perfectionism began to emerge over the next two centuries. An early sign was the materialism of Hobbes which came to the conclusion that a mechanical and deterministic explanation of life meant there was no true justice or moral law. Nature was a state of warfare, and the only security for individuals was in their surrender to a sovereign power. Likewise, Rousseau challenged the universal standards of reason proclaimed by the Enlightenment. He declared that human worth depends not upon intelligence but upon moral nature, which consists essentially of feeling. Humans are equal by nature, civilization has corrupted them with the institutions that enslave them. It is significant, Polanyi points out, that the solution for both Hobbes and Rousseau was in a voluntary surrender of individual will to the absolute will of the state, even though Hobbes spoke for a monarchy and Rousseau for a democracy. These arguments suggest "that when revolutions demanding total individual liberty were eventually to lead to the establishment of a collectivist absolutism, these logical implications were actually at work in the process."[28]

On the surface, the optimism of the Enlightenment appeared to continue in the nineteenth century. "The performance of the eighteenth century had been intellectual, the progress of the nineteenth century was moral and sentient. It produced our modern Western civilization: a society that was with all its evils, more free and more humane than any that had existed before."[29] This liberal impulse seeking freedom, justice, and equality and attacking social evils with indignation continued to effect change and to improve society generally until the First World War. But the undercurrent of doubt of the universal standards of reason, indicated by Hobbes and Rousseau, continued. It began to be apparent that the Enlightenment confidence in reason could not be justified in light of its own skeptical views. The idea began to spread that science, the guide to moral progress, actually demonstrates that moral claims are illusory.

The struggle with these doubts can be seen in three instances. First, in science itself a new positivist philosophy arose denying that scientific theories had any claim to inherent rationality. Such claims for rationality were now to be regarded as metaphysical and mystical. This new view was energetically set forth by Ernst Mach, founder of the Vienna school of positivism. According to Mach, scientific theories are only convenient summaries of empirical data, labor-saving devices, mental constructs for clarifying observations. Since such scientific concepts are incapable of empirical observation, they are not to be regarded as real. Consequently, scientific theory is denied all persuasive power in itself. One must go to experience, or to sense data, to affirm anything. Whenever an empirical observation arises that contradicts a theory, the theory should be dropped immediately. These views, Polanyi notes, can be traced back to Locke and Hume. They are the logical consequences of the mechanist separation of experience and theory. This positivist model is the one that has dominated the twentieth century's thinking on science.

The second outbreak against the rationalism of the Enlightenment came in the form of Romantic individualism anticipated by Rousseau. This is the idea of the modern individual, a person unique and autonomous. On one side, this movement produced a renewal of the arts, an expression of creativity and imagination. On the other side, it foreshadowed the moral nihilist. Turgenev,

Dostoevsky, and Nietzsche foresaw and represented this event. Turgenev portrayed the student Bazarov as a nihilist and had him declare that "a nihilist is the man who bows to no authority. . . . There is no single institution of our society which should not be destroyed."[30] Dostoevsky realized that science had destroyed the conception of moral responsibility and depicted characters who demonstrated their independent will by committing suicide or murder. Nietzsche, in agreement with Dostoevsky, showed that modern skepticism had destroyed the grounds of all accepted values and projected a superior man, respecting no laws, ready for violence beyond good and evil. What these writers conveyed on paper as a warning became a widespread conviction, namely, that evil is more honest than good because it cannot be suspected of hypocrisy.

The third reaction to the collapse of the Enlightenment came in an attempt to rescue its political and scientific ideals. With universal reason in doubt, Hegel constructed a systematic approach making reason immanent in history. Polanyi views Hegel as having given reason a safe but redundant home, since the course of history would be understood in Hegel's thought as the working out of reason. The next step was made by Marx and Engels, who completed the disestablishment of reason by inverting Hegel's dialectic and replacing it with a material principle of history. This substitution of economic materialism for reason invested Marxism with its sense of scientific certainty. At the same time, the sense of the course of economic conflict following a scientific principle gave it a moral feeling of righteousness. Marx, as is well known, saw history as determined by the necessity of class wars that bring successive improvements in the modes of production. The moral principles of each period being determined by the interests of the ruling glass, there was no need to try for reform by appeals to justice and brotherhood. Nor was there any point in following moral principles in carrying out a revolution that was historically inevitable. Marxism in this way gave a scientific ideology that had the moral aims of a classless society, yet these aims were not

[22]

exposed to skepticism because they were embodied in the mechanism of material progress itself.

The pattern of the objective ideal of knowledge which grew from the time of the scientific revolution is now complete. We have seen how it at first became established as the method of science and how it led to humanitarian benefits. We have also seen that it was composed of elements which inevitably led to contradictions and instabilities in the societies that followed the scientific outlook. We now have four results. First, the objective ideal remains our dominant view of knowledge despite the consequences of our century of suffering. It seems that people have not sufficiently seen the connection between the behavior of our age and its ideas. If it is pointed out that impersonal objective knowledge is impossible because we all have a bias, the argument is taken as motivation to work harder and to try to be more scientific and to eliminate our personal participation as a defect. The ideal of scientific detachment appears to survive unshaken by our experience. Second, the world of science itself has retreated in its theory of knowledge to the recording of sense data and has refused to comprehend its observations as pointers to a world of actual order and rationality. The once stable laws of Newton are now the projections of our consciousness upon a chance universe. Third, we have in one line of reaction to the Enlightenment the basis for extravagant individualism. Fourth, we have also in the same moral inversion the basis for the politics of violence.

The complexity and the detail, the abundance of evidence and historical examples cited by Polanyi, are barely surveyed here. We have tried to see the outline of his analysis. If the account is successful, we can see the objective ideal of knowledge in what is happening today, in the oscillation of youth between personal immoralism and social violence, in the acceptance of the realpolitik that power makes right, in the cynical view that courts dispense favors and have no true justice, in the contempt of academics for the quest for ultimate meaning, in the clinical reports of laboratories that experiment on human beings without their subjects' knowing the full implications, in the pornographic exploration of life in literature and mass media, in the outbreaks of bombing, kidnapping, and murdering of innocent persons to right wrongs.

A vast range of senseless actions flow from a world in which humans are separated from themselves by the contradiction between moral obligation and moral skepticism, which follows from the mechanical view of reality. Polanyi lays bare the central dogma of the scientific outlook, the dogma that knowledge is based on what cannot be doubted and what can be empirically observed. The crucial question then becomes whether or not this objective ideal of knowledge is true in practice. Does genuine knowledge proceed from doubt? Does science accept as true only what can be empirically demonstrated? Unless we can radically change and re-establish the grounds of scientific and of human knowledge, our situation is likely to worsen.

THE EXAMPLE OF SCIENTIFIC DISCOVERY

Throughout we have tried to maintain a distinction between the content and process of science and the objective ideal of knowledge. Polanyi believes in and respects the methods of science but disagrees with the view that is projected about them. Scientific results could not be achieved, he says, if this model were strictly followed. The model of the objective ideal is one widely assumed by and disastrously influential upon scientists and the public, yet it is a model that is impossible to follow in practice. Once this fact is understood, we shall be free to move to a new understanding, one that will give us grounds for uniting human responsibility and our methods of knowing.

The most direct way to test the objective ideal of knowledge is to examine the nature of scientific discovery.[31] We pay our highest tributes to science and its heroes for their capacity to enlighten and to widen our horizons of knowledge. If scientific discovery is based upon the objective ideal, the objective ideal has a persuasive case. If scientific discovery works in a way contradictory to the objective ideal, then we are compelled to find the method by which it achieves its results so that we may more accurately teach and employ the method of science.

Where does scientific discovery begin? That appears to be an easier question to answer than it really is. One of the more commonplace facts of scientific life is that there is no sure way to making discoveries. In the absence of a precise answer, we can try to find the conditions under which scientific discoveries occur and are established. One obvious component is a trained scientist equipped with the tools for doing research. Such a condition immediately turns out to be nonobjective. A trained scientist working in a laboratory is a person prepared by years of intensive training and with a devotion to his subject that shows a strong personal commitment and belief. But even if the scientist could be considered objective in the background and preparation for his work, there is still another condition that is also crucial, that is, the choosing of a scientific problem.

The choice of a problem affects directly the chances of discovery. Significant discoveries can only come from significant problems. Yet, significant problems are not always clear until significant discoveries have followed from them. How can one tell in advance that a problem is significant and has high discovery potential? Consider, for example, the difficulty of seeing in advance the implications of Copernicus's work. When he died, he had no knowledge that his mathematical astronomy would lead to a revolution in our total intellectual understanding. He was aware that his work was controversial, especially religiously, but the importance of his work was to unfold in the next hundred and fifty years, leading up to Newton's triumph. Or, more in our context, consider the difficulty of estimating the value of Einstein's theory of relativity in advance of its discovery. Such cases point to an ambiguity at the center of the scientific process and suggest that the

[25]

objective criterion does not apply to scientific discovery. If this criterion does not apply here, how does science make discoveries and add so wonderfully to our understanding?

The importance of discovery is almost completely neglected in contemporary philosophy of science. The emphasis is placed upon the procedures followed within routine science and on following up a promising problem, data, or hunch once these foundations have been attained. The decisive question of gaining a starting point is ignored. In fact, one of the most widely-read authorities on the subject of scientific discovery regards the origin of creative scientific ideas as irrelevant.[32] Such a view allows him and others to avoid the problem of the objective ideal of knowledge and to live in the illusion of its truth. The nature of discovery is the Achilles' heel of the objective ideal of knowledge. Once this issue is seen, the paradigm begins to fall and an alternative view begins to arise.

Polanyi's experience as a physical chemist had taught him that the strictness and rigor of scientific procedure were secondary to the role of the creative imagination. Scientific work cannot be carried out by mere following of rules. At every step, there are questions of personal judgment that go beyond the rules. These are judgments that demand insight and understanding. Two scientists could have a perfectly identical understanding of scientific laws and theories, but one may make a great discovery and the other spend his or her life doing ordinary research which conforms to current knowledge. The difference lies in the personal judgment of the scientist.

What is the nature of creative imagination that produces scientific discoveries?[33] Polanyi found the clue in Gestalt psychology, but he carried it further. Gestalt psychology had claimed that our knowledge seemed to be the integration of certain bits in our perception to form a whole. This recognition of pattern had an affinity to the problem of scientific discovery where the researcher is engaged in the problem of trying to find the coherence of various pieces of information. While Gestalt psychology had stopped at a more mechanistic point and had regarded perception to be an internal equilibration of external stimuli, Polanyi added that the seeing of a pattern is the outcome of an intentional effort of the person to find order in reality. The implications of this insight were far-reaching. It meant that not only was the act of discovery dependent upon our personal powers of thought, but it overthrew three centuries of epistemology that had built upon a structure of knowledge in which there was no person. The most basic assumptions of our idea of knowledge were challenged by the notion that our knowing is an integration of bodily clues that we indwell in order to understand.

Polanyi began to collect cases in which the most traditional scientific rules were flouted. He became, as he says, "a scandal-monger," showing that it was not to the advantage of science to follow its dogma of objective knowledge. One of his most striking cases was the story of Einstein's discovery of the theory of relativity.[34] According to most physics textbooks, Einstein was led to his theory by the failure of the famous Michelson and Morley experiment of 1887, an experiment which expected to find that a light signal sent out from a given point would be affected by the motion of the earth. However, the experiment showed no discrepancy regardless of the direction of the measurement. Working from the objective ideal of knowledge which holds that science works from observable facts, textbooks say that Einstein set out to find a new conception of space and time to explain the Michelson and Morley experiment. Actually, Einstein himself indicated in his autobiography that the new theory was primarily a work of his imagination. When he was a schoolboy of sixteen years, he had already begun to ponder intuitively the problem of relativity. Polanyi confirmed this statement by Einstein by personal letter and included the confirmation in *Personal Knowledge* in 1958. Despite the evidence the dogma persisted, and in 1963 a prominent philosopher of science said that Polanyi's account was pure invention and that Polanyi's description of Einstein's discovery "was like Schiller's story that his poetic inspiration came to him by smelling rotten apples."[35] In 1969, eleven years later, Gerald Holton confirmed again Polanyi's story of Einstein's discovery with evidence based upon Einstein's personal papers.[36]

The importance of discovery reaches far beyond the obvious

point of making discoveries themselves. Following through the nature of discovery, we are led to a total rethinking of the general ideal of knowledge in our culture. Discovery is the point within science itself that leads to a truer understanding of knowledge and of ourselves as persons. Our course now is to follow Polanyi from the unfolding of the nature of discovery in science to a new theory of knowledge. This process itself must contend with our habitual method of doubt and with the impossibility of making a radical change in world view on the basis of a single argument. Yet, Polanyi gives a breadth of connections and evidence. Once the scope of his argument is surveyed, the basis for this new theory is convincing.

ii. From Scientist to Philosopher

THE ONLY GENUINE INTEREST

When Polanyi received in 1959 the Le Comte du Nouy Foundation Award for his book *Personal Knowledge,* he revealed a distinctive quality of wonder and imagination that characterizes his life. He said:

I have been often asked why I gave up my work in chemistry in favor of economics, sociology, philosophy, and the like. The answer is really quite simple: a desire to go back to normal. We all started with being interested in the whole world; it's the only genuine interest we can have.[1]

The breadth and depth of Polanyi's knowledge and understanding are truly among the outstanding achievements of men of this century. As the reader of his works finds, he commands a technical understanding of many major areas of intellectual study today, including the arts as well as the social and physical sciences. This comprehensiveness grew from his native intellectual gifts, combined with a constant devotion to life as intrinsically profound and interesting. Polanyi seems to be a man perpetually fascinated by the ranges of reality that come to us through our experience. He sees a richness and elegance opening up and beckoning us. Hence, he has felt at home wherever he could address himself to the task of responding to the greatness of life. His own words point the way to seeing his philosophical development. The whole world is his only genuine interest.

He may have forsaken the honor of the highest prizes in science by his changing to social thought and philosophy. At least his scientific work was considered outstanding, with numerous international awards, and two of his students, who are Nobel laureates, have generously praised Polanyi for the contribution he made to their careers.[2] These distinguished leaders of science and thought indicate Polanyi's greatness in their tributes to the loftiness that occupied his scientific career. His work was always a medium through which he pursued the fundamental issues of the time. Even persons who were criticized in their thought by Polanyi could see that his aim was to seek the truth constructively. In 1965, he made a scathing attack upon a leading American sociologist for his sanguine endorsement of a "value free" textbook. Yet in 1973, the same sociologist graciously sent him a copy of a *Festschrift* marking the effect of his own life's work on society, and he inscribed the book as follows: "For Michael, Master of us all in the field we try to cultivate."[3] This esteem rises from Polanyi's earnest concern about the whole world, a concern that pervades his entire life. As we trace the lines of his career and ideas, we will need to keep this glimpse of Polanyi at the LeComte du Nouy ceremony in mind. Repeatedly Polanyi will be contending against the views that make life seem pedestrian and rob it of its vitality. His critique of the influence of the scientific bewitchment of our time is that it is taking away from us the most interesting and promising aspects of life.

Another person tells us about the size of life that Polanyi sought from his earliest years. As a university student in Budapest, Polanyi was a founder and member of a student society known as the

Galileo Circle. The group pursued the theme of science above all in its daily discussions of politics and of the existence of God. A progressive-minded student society, the Galileo Circle was imbued with the radical rationalism of revolutionaries. In this setting, Michael Polanyi was a wise and balanced member, anticipating his later concern for traditional rather than radical reforms. Remembering this period, Paul Ignotus describes Polanyi's "liberality of mind, the simultaneity of personal and technical interests, and the ability to coordinate them in behavior as well as in philosophy." Then Ignotus adds, "What made him differ most from those around him was his reverence."[4]

The actual professional careers of Polanyi are four in number: medicine, physical chemistry, social science, and philosophy. His intellectual competence, his breadth of knowledge, and his intimate experience with intellectual and social issues have given him a vantage point for producing an original and penetrating view of our situation. It is perhaps fortunate that he did not begin in philosophy, in order that he could gain perspective on our philosophical problems first hand. By coming from the outside, he brought a range and grasp that make his thought the most comprehensive and experienced treatment of the problem of knowledge today. Such words even betray his scope, for he never saw the problem of knowledge as an academic problem alone. It was always the question of the nature of our knowing and of its bearing upon the major issues of our life and destiny. His genuine interest in the whole world led Polanyi to professional achievement in difficult and distinctive fields, and the inclusiveness of his experience equipped him to fathom the central problem of our beliefs and actions.

INDUCTION INTO SCIENCE

Polanyi entered science with philosophical and moral concern. He came from a talented and intellectual family in Budapest. When he entered the university there in 1908, he went with the enthusiasm and commitment of those intellectuals who sought through science and reason to improve the condition of the world. Within two years after his entrance, at the age of nineteen, he published his first scientific paper, "Chemistry of the Hydrocephalic Liquid." Three years later in 1913, he graduated with a degree in medicine. At that time his hopes were to practice medicine, to engage in scientific research, and to read widely on questions of social and political significance.

The outbreak of the First World War led in a curious way to Polanyi's deeper involvement in scientific research. In 1913 and 1914 he published a number of scientific papers in Hungarian and German scientific journals on applications of the quantum theory of thermodynamics and on the thermodynamics of adsorption. When he entered the Austro-Hungarian army in 1914 as a medical officer, these interests in physical chemistry continued. Working overtime, the young medical officer wrote to the already world-renowned physicist Albert Einstein concerning his scientific conjectures. Impressed by the quality of the unknown army officer's mind, Einstein responded in copious notes written in longhand. Then Polanyi was afflicted by diphtheria, and he was forced to rest to regain his health. During his convalescence, Polanyi began to develop his ideas into a thesis, "The Adsorption of Gases by a Solid Non-Volatile Adsorbent." The thesis was accepted in 1916, a Ph.D. in physical chemistry was granted the following year, and after the war Polanyi continued research in physical chemistry. But the sequel of his move into physical chemistry demonstrates one of the features of scientific practice, namely, its rule by orthodoxy and the limitation of dissent.

The success of Polanyi's thesis on the potential theory of adsorption was short-lived.[5] The turmoil of the war had protected his theory from the knowledge of experiments that would have made it untenable. Soon he was invited by the great Fritz Haber to give a full explanation of his theory before the Kaiser Wilhelm Institute for Physical Chemistry in Berlin. Einstein was also especially invited to attend and to comment on Polanyi's lecture. The results were nearly disastrous for Polanyi's career. Both Haber and Einstein opposed Polanyi's theory on the grounds that he had displayed a total disregard for the new knowledge of the electrical concept of interatomic forces. Polanyi persisted with further evidence at a later meeting, but his theory was rejected again as a failure. If Polanyi had not gone on immediately to prove himself in other work in physical chemistry, the opposition to his theory would have ended his scientific career. Still, the most striking point to the story is the fact that Polanyi's theory was right and is in use today. The evidence to confirm the theory began to appear in 1930, and others went on to establish what Polanyi had begun. Far from teaching that science is practiced by a strict code of impartiality and openness, the episode discloses the role of authority in the work of science.

Polanyi himself does not believe that the mistaken rejection of his work represents a fault in the nature of science. On the contrary, it is an example of the necessary guidance of science by adherence to current standards of scientific knowledge and by the weight of opinion exercised by scientific leaders. The direct implications of this experience are counter to the accepted belief that science grows by a simple following of facts. Discoveries are made by the efforts of persons who believe in their work, but the acceptance of discoveries also requires a readiness to believe within the scientific community. Even specific evidence cannot always counter the established views. By this rule of orthodoxy, science risks ignoring important work, but it also guards against being flooded with nonsense.

Polanyi recorded the lessons of his experience with the potential theory of adsorption in 1963 in an article in *Science*. He concluded by contrasting the facts of his work with the following statement by Bertrand Russell:

The triumphs of science are due to the substitution of observation and inference for authority. Every attempt to revive authority in intellectual matters is a retrograde step. And it is part of the scientific attitude that the pronouncements of science do not claim to be certain, but only the most probable basis of present evidence.

One of the great benefits that science confers upon those who understand its spirit is that it enables them to live without the delusive support of subjective authority.[6]

Russell's statement represents the kind of view that has misrepresented the actual nature of scientific process and has taught the public to believe that science is completely objective. From experience Polanyi knew this view to be mistaken.

It was only a brief period after Polanyi went to Berlin before he became a recognized and established leader in physical chemistry. The story of this success also bore lessons on the nature of scientific knowledge and discovery that he would recall later.[7] In 1920, he was appointed to the Kaiser Wilhelm Institute for Fiber Chemistry. During Polanyi's orientation and introduction to the several associated research institutes there, Fritz Haber chided Polanyi for trying to solve too large a problem in his work on reaction velocity and advised him instead "to cook a piece of meat." Soon the opportunity was given by Reginald Oliver Herzog, director of the Fiber Chemistry Institute. Polanyi was asked to solve the mystery of an X-ray diffraction pattern in "a bundle of ramie fibers." Although the theory of X-ray diffraction was new to him, Polanyi came up with the solution quickly. This success proved to be the "piece of meat" he needed "to cook." His position at the Institute was transformed. Herzog showered him with every facility for experimental work, including funds for employing assistants and research students. Besides reminding him of the importance of personal authority in science, this stage also added an insight into the way science solves problems by taking seriously its own current tradition and sense of what are fitting problems. "Discovery requires in fact something beyond craftsmanship, namely the gift of recognizing a problem that is ripe for solution by your own powers, large enough to engage your powers to the full, and worth the expenditure of effort."[8] Such judgments are the kind that are not reducible to exact rules or formulas and demand a theory of knowledge that includes them in the central work of science.

The achievements of Polanyi at the Institute for Fiber Chemistry led to his promotion in 1923 to full membership in the Kaiser Wilhelm Institute for Physical Chemistry, but his scientific research never excluded his interest in the problems of the times. Always aware of the interactions of science and society, he formed in 1928 with Leo Szilard, Eugene Wigner, and John Von Neumann a discussion group on Soviet affairs. The political developments in Russia and in Germany were to have a direct impact upon Polanyi's life within a few years.

THE FREEDOM OF SCIENCE

The years in Berlin at the Kaiser Wilhelm Institute were stimulating and creative years. Polanyi attained international distinction, and in 1933 when he resigned his position in protest against Hitler's policies, he was immediately invited to a chair in physical chemistry at the University of Manchester in England. The political turmoil of Europe continued to press upon Polanyi in his new position. The conflicts between rival systems began to alert him to the deeper philosophical problems that were involved. The conflicts were about ideas and values, not power only. In 1935 a conversation with Bukharin, a leading Communist theoretician, in Russia gave him a decisive clue to the problem. Bukharin told Polanyi that the pursuit of pure science "was a morbid symptom of a class society; under socialism the conception of science pursued for its own sake would disappear, for the interests of scientists would spontaneously turn to problems of the current Five-Year Plan."[9] Polanyi was struck by the fact that independent scientific thought was being denied by a socialist theory that based itself upon its scientific appeal. To Polanyi it seemed that paradoxically the scientific outlook had produced a mechanical conception of human nature and history in which there were no grounds for science itself.

The years 1935 and 1936 were germinal ones in Polanyi's philosophical formulations. Two major seeds of his ideas were articulated in his publications. One idea reflects his visits to the Soviet Union with a critique of the fact that there was no widespread recognition that the Communists had returned to free market practices in certain aspects. Contrary to popular reports, Polanyi found the Soviet economic system to be a system of planned production, not planned economy.[10] The difference between the two forms of planning is enormous. Planned production sets goals but allows for flexibility and changes throughout the system to occur without requiring central control of all decisions. Planned economy presumes that total production and distribution can be centrally controlled. The significance of this difference is to show the failure of the Communist attempt at centralized government control of all economic activities. Polanyi notes that Lenin had actually abandoned the ideal of a Communist economy in 1921 after the famine of that year. This failure is more serious because it demonstrates the flaw in the mistaken view of science on which Communism rests. The Communists had believed originally in an objectification and precision in science that neglected the crucial roles of personal judgment and mutual adjustment. This was a lack of understanding of the way science and other rationally ordered communities pursued problem solving effectively. Later Polanyi defined this process in his conception of "polycentric tasks," the spontaneous ordering of mutually coordinated activities.[11] This idea foreshadows Polanyi's major contribution to the understanding of the roles of tradition and of community in scientific discovery.

The second idea, expressed then and later to bloom into a major philosophical component of his theory of knowledge, was the importance of ambiguity in science. Characteristically, it appears in a response of Polanyi to what others were saying about the nature of science, statements that he found to contradict the integrity of science and his own experience. After reading arguments in philosophy of science on the precision of the scientific process, Polanyi countered with a brief discussion of "The Value of the Inexact." Some of his seminal ideas appeared here in incipient

[36]

form. A lengthy extract, almost the whole response itself, shows Polanyi's anticipation of his later concept of "tacit knowing."

The subject of chemical concepts as opposed to physical ones has always been fascinating to me because it shows the great value of inexact ideas. . . . Of course, the mere fact that there is no absolute security for the validity of what we consider exact natural laws should lead to the conclusion that these laws are only valuable in combination with the element of uncertainty in them, which is compensated by the supreme sanction of validity, which is faith. . . . There is not a single rule in chemistry which is not qualified by important exceptions. The character of a substance or class of substances is as complex as the features of physiognomy and the art of chemistry appears to be the power of being aware of these complex attitudes of matter, and in a thousand delicate attempts to add further evidence to, and enlarge the field of this awareness; thus, were a million compounds synthesized it would be an achievement which could never have been attained by exact methods. . . . I think it is good to contemplate how useless, or even harmful exactitude becomes at so close quarters to physics. Just link up two or three of the atoms of physics, and their behavior becomes so complex as to be beyond the range of exactitude. How supremely unreasonable it appears then, to claim that, by precise measurements and mathematical treatment, i.e. physical exactitude, a vital knowledge and command of such objects as living organisms and social bodies should be found. All these fields of high complexity gain real profit only from the discovery of specific tendencies of behavior incorporated in their functional outlines.[12]

Here are nearly all the major themes of Polanyi's later epistemology, from the nature of recognition of pattern to the understanding of living beings. These ideas were to be nurtured by the political and social conflicts of the period.

The crisis of philosophy and science became more acute to Polanyi's eyes in 1937. Reporting in *Nature* on an international scientific meeting at the Congrès du Palais de la Découverte in

Paris, he perceived the growing threat of totalitarian ideologies to science.[13] Jean Perrin, Minister of Education, opened the meeting with a declaration of "science as the new supreme religion destined to reign over the happy future." Then the minister turned to the introduction of the delegates by their countries, and the refutation of his remarks occurred. Japan and the Soviet Union had sent no delegates. The Germans were worried about their relations to France. The Italians were afraid to mention politics. There were loud cheers of support for the delegates from Spain. By the time the list of introductions was finished, this occasion had illustrated the new situation of science in the world. "Science, and generally the independent search for truth is destroyed when political liberty falls."

The following year Polanyi joined in the founding of the Society for the Freedom of Science in opposition to the centralization of scientific planning. A wide number of scientific leaders in England had already developed a movement for the central planning of science. The centralization movement already had been instituted in 1931 at the International Congress of the History of Science in London. By 1939, it had developed an articulate program and following. The arguments for it were made from utilitarian and positivistic assumptions.

Hogben's *Science for the Citizen* and Bernal's *Social Functions of Science* were representative of the ideas of the movement for centrally planned science. They took as their chief example the success of central planning in the Soviet Union, oblivious to the actual modifications that it had to undergo. They contended that the primary function of science is to promote human welfare and that pure scientific research should be discontinued. They claimed that pure science is a fiction since all real science arises in answer to the needs of society. Because modern science has erroneously pursued the ideal of pure science, all science should be brought under a central authority in the interests of society. Responsible scientists should organize themselves politically and work to establish the central planning of science.

So generally did these ideas gain acceptance that even the author-

[38]

itative scientific journal *Nature* supported planned science momentarily and provoked the following passionate response from Polanyi: "I, for one, can recognize nothing more holy than scientific truth, and consider it a danger to science and humanity if the pursuit of pure science, regardless of society, is denied by a representative organ of science."[14]

To Polanyi the freedom of science controversy represented the same issues that were involved in the growing international struggle against the totalitarian regimes, respect for truth and thought. Soon after arriving in England from Germany, he had spoken of the the decreasing grounds for freedom of thought and argument.[15] Many thinkers, he observed, no longer believed in truth, and of the few who did, still fewer considered it right to tell the truth regardless of the consequences. The effect of this loss was that thinkers forfeited their right to restrain governments by appeals to truth. Power and its weapon, propaganda, were becoming the determiners of human lives.

The freedom of science controversy helped to synthesize the philosophical ideas of Polanyi and to lead him deeper into the problem of knowledge. Against the caricature of the pure scientist whimsically or selfishly pursuing his own interests, Polanyi placed the picture of the scientist in an autonomous but responsible community. This self-government is made possible by a set of shared beliefs. The process of scientific development is an illustration of this self-regulating framework. The primary decisions in making scientific progress are made by individuals. These individuals are usually trained by professional scientists who have been accredited by other scientists as competent. Furthermore, the scientific community as a whole is accredited by the public as competent and valuable. The public could—as some portions still do—choose to support a magical or astrological view of reality. In such ways, the individual scientist is a member of a community of shared beliefs whose leaders in important scientific institutions have accredited him or her as trustworthy and competent to be given the freedom to pursue his or her own lines of inquiry.

The freedom of the individual scientist and the steps of scientific

[39]

research are also governed by a general framework of beliefs. The selection of a scientific problem for investigation is influenced by the state of knowledge and existing standards of science at that time. The possible steps to be taken toward the solution of a problem are also regulated by the current status of knowledge and interests in science. This form of self-regulation and guidance gives both a measure of definiteness and indeterminacy in scientific research and accounts for the phenomenon of simultaneous discoveries. At a given moment several scientists may be working independently on the same problem and arrive at virtually the same conclusion because they follow independently the current beliefs and standards of the scientific community. Finally, the evaluation of the individual's scientific results depends upon the judgment of the scientific community and, in turn, upon the response of the public.

Such a network of beliefs and practices develops a lively and subtle tradition whose operations and premises can never be completely defined. For the most part, these beliefs and premises are embodied in the example of the scientific community. So indefinable are these principles that they can only be transmitted personally by scientists who work with apprentices. This ineffable quality of science explains why the growth of science has depended upon leaders from the older scientific centers going to new centers, or students going to the established centers to do advanced research. Instead of resembling an operation of exact and precise principles that can be organized and directed by a central authority, scientific research is more like an art, the art of making certain kinds of discoveries.

Throughout these arguments with the world of politics and of scientific administration, Polanyi continued to be a leading physical chemist. An appraisal of his work as a physical chemist indicates an achievement of at least thirty-nine major contributions and discoveries and the publication of over two hundred scientific papers before Polanyi turned full-time to philosophy.[16]

One gathers from the volume of Polanyi's scientific and social-philosophical papers that his life was intense and preoccupied almost constantly with questions of substance. Nobel laureate Melvin Calvin, who was Polanyi's student in 1935, says that Polanyi was never content to be doing one thing but always was carrying on a number of investigations simultaneously.[17] During the years 1933–48, Polanyi not only produced significant works in science and social thought, but also entered the field of economics and produced major works there. He particularly wrote on themes of free trade, unemployment and money, and patent reform. His ideas in this area were not only widely circulated but also included the making of a film on teaching economics by motion symbols.[18]

Polanyi's scientific eminence, combined with his sense of social and philosophical responsibility, led him into serious dialogue with major thinkers. In 1939, Joseph Oldham, a distinguished ecumenical leader, invited Polanyi to join the company of other leading thinkers to discuss the basic questions facing our civilization.[19] Numbered among this group called "The Moot" were Karl Mannheim, Sir Walter Moberly, T. S. Eliot, H. A. Hodges, Kathleen Bliss, A. R. Vidler, D. M. MacKinnon, and John Baillie. Apart from his personal experience as a scientist and thinker, Polanyi regarded the biannual meetings of this society as a major intellectual influence on his thought.

When the end of the war came in 1945, the movement to centralize science had abated. Polanyi addressed the British Association for the Advancement of Science on the topic "Social Message of Pure Science."[20] He identified the roots of the attack on the independence of scientific thought as the modern materialistic analysis, moral skepticism, and moral passion. The meeting showed itself consistently in favor of the traditional position of pure science. The freedom of science had been preserved, and Polanyi had irrevocably become a genuine philosopher. Like a Socrates driven by the moral crisis of his time, he had been compelled to ask the basic questions about the nature of knowledge and of the good. The fruits of his search were to lead him into further conflict with the dominant philosophies of the age.

THE INAUGURAL ADDRESS

The change of Polanyi's central intellectual interest was recognized by the University of Manchester in 1948 when it made an unusual arrangement for him to exchange his chair in physical chemistry for one in social thought, free of teaching duties. While the official acknowledgment came in 1948, the systematic development of Polanyi's philosophy began in 1946 when he was fifty-five years old. Prior to this time, the philosophical investigations of Polanyi had been more circumstantial, the response to specific issues that he faced.

In 1946 Polanyi set forth for the first time a general outline of his philosophy in the Riddell Lectures at the University of Durham. Published as *Science, Faith and Society*, these lectures could be called an inaugural address for a post-critical philosophy.[21] They were only the beginning of a program that would occupy him for the rest of his life. Striking is the fact that this presentation does not address itself strictly to problems of epistemology but to the total human situation in an age of science. Yet the problems of the nature of scientific knowledge and our application of it form the main issue.

At the heart of these lectures is the nature of scientific discovery. From the start, Polanyi takes the way science establishes its results as decisive. The important thing about science is that it enables us to make contact with reality in a way that is continuously fruitful and interesting. Science is a way of knowing that has opened up vast domains to us, and Polanyi's aim is to understand and to foster this method. His argument for science is also a refutation of the objective ideal of scientific knowledge. Instead of being the principal features of science, exactness and precision, impersonality and detachment are relative terms whose usefulness depends upon a larger foundation of beliefs and acceptances that are prior to them.

The first of the three lectures traces the unformalizable qualities of science and shows that these tacit components play an essential role in the scientific process. For example, Polanyi shows that we could never discover natural laws if the discovery depended entirely

[42]

upon the application of exact rules of procedure. We might have all relevant experience in terms of a list of figures so that mass, time, position, velocities, wave lengths, and so on were represented. Yet, we could not from this vast amount of exact information derive a single scientific law. There would be an infinite number of possible relations between these figures. Before a natural law could be attained there would have to be three components present.

The first component is the art of guessing right. Here Polanyi is referring to what is commonly known as a hypothesis, but he elucidates the fact that a good hypothesis is a creative act and closer to art than to rule-following. The hypothesis or guess makes an assumption that there is present in the data a reality capable of being known, and it selects from a nearly infinite number of possibilities the explanation that seems most likely. In this manner, the array of information is brought toward intelligibility.

The second component needed to find a natural law is skill in looking at the unknown. How does science grasp correctly a reality that is not yet known? The answer is suggested to Polanyi by Gestalt psychology. We perceive reality first in terms of a coherent outline or pattern. Through our awareness of this outline, we are given the reality of an object intimated but not fully known. The advantage of the scientist is his skill, gained from training and example, in guessing what reality is implied in a given pattern. The scientist excels in his ability to recognize and to integrate clues about reality that are hidden or only dimly perceived at first. The suggestion from Gestalt psychology will later be carried into deeper and more radical implications. Here it forms a part of Polanyi's demonstration that scientific understanding is not simply a matter of doing experiments and recording observations. The reduction of scientific method to only observation and testing falsely implies that scientific discovery occurs mainly through reliance upon known phenomena. Polanyi is pointing to how our reliance upon known phenomena enables us to intuit patterns of previously unknown realities. In this respect, scientific discovery is akin to the vision that guides the work of art. "The process resembles the creation of a work of art which is firmly guided by the

[43]

final whole even though the whole can be definitely conceived only in terms of its yet undiscovered particulars. . . ."[22] Such is the history of great scientific discoveries. Copernicus, Newton, Darwin, Einstein, Dalton, and many others achieved discoveries whose predictions were only confirmed years later. In each case, the scientist was guided by an interpretation of clues to see a reality not yet seen by others.

The third component in finding a natural law in a cluster of information is the foundation of the first two given; it is the standard of scientific validity itself. The individual scientist operates from personal intuitions formed within a society that interprets nature in a scientific way. Polanyi reminds us that there are primitive societies still in existence that do not accept our common generalizations that we regard as scientific fact, and no amount of argument can persuade them to change their minds. The validity of science rests upon a preference of interpretation developed over hundreds of years by our civilization. From birth to research, the individual scientist is instilled with the convictions of science. In his laboratory, he is guided not only by the specific techniques and rules of his work but also by the scientific premises given to him in his general experience and education.

In the second lecture, Polanyi continues his assault upon the citadel of scientific objectivity by demonstrating another major area that is not subject to precise rules and measurement, namely the government of science itself. Drawing upon his years of experience in science, Polanyi develops a picture of science as a republic bound together by loyalty to a common tradition and conscience. It is this republic that is responsible for the transmission of its premises and their administration.

Induction into this republic begins, as we have seen, with the birth and then the cultural education of the young scientist, who is taught our basic assumptions about nature. The purpose of later scientific training is to enable the student to establish contact with the reality to which scientific knowledge is a clue. After the apprentice has internalized the tradition of science, he or she begins to replace the authority of the teacher and textbooks with the greater authority of scientific reality itself. The apprentice becomes an independent scientist relying on his or her own personal judgment which is governed by the authority of the reality seen by all scientists.

Besides governing through the development of a sense of scientific conscience, the republic of science also governs by its administration of standards and materials. One form of this discipline and control is the scientific publication. The publication is a means of checking, testing, and accepting scientific reports. What is printed depends upon the approval of editorial referees. Wide acceptance eventually leads to incorporation into textbooks where the essential doctrines of science are summarized. Another regulative force is the prestige and influence of major scientific posts—university chairs, research grants, prizes, and leadership of institutes. Finally, the republic is guided by a sense of what is scientifically valuable. A scientific discovery, to be valuable, must be not only valid but interesting. An accurate measurement of water flowing in the gutter of a street, says Polanyi, is not necessarily a contribution to science. A valuable scientific discovery has relevance to the current status of scientific knowledge.

The nature of the shared convictions that govern the scientific community is seen particularly in the way controversy is handled. When controversy arises, the republic of science appeals to tradition as interpreted by the conscience of the community. Tradition is the ground for both the criticism and the appeal of new discoveries. New claims are judged by what is known, and the expounder of new views appeals to the community on the basis that his work is the bearer of a deeper and more true understanding of the tradition. Because scientific controversy is resolved by reference to a common tradition, there is continuity instead of discontinuity in scientific innovation. This loyalty to a living tradition illuminates the phenomenon of a general unanimity in the republic of science.

Throughout these lectures, Polanyi points to the extensive proportions of scientific work that function more like maxims than strict rules. In the third and final lecture, Polanyi widens the understanding of scientific practice by discussing the premises of the free society upon which it depends. While science is seen as a network of only partly definable assumptions taught and held by its community, it is also upheld by certain basic premises of the society that developed it.

The first of the premises is the belief in obtaining the truth by free discussion and free inquiry. Every scientist is a part of the government of science and participates in the formulation of ongoing scientific understanding. There is no absolute central authority to arbitrate controversy. Issues are settled by debating them in the forum of scientific opinion. This manner of settling disputes and establishing consensus is a heritage common to our general democratic institutions.

A second and corollary premise is a belief in the reality of the truth and in our obligation and capacity to discover it. A community that resolves its disputes by free discussion and inquiry is dependent upon the belief that humans can recognize and share a rational and universal standard. The esteem in which science is held is partly due to its practice of this belief. Our society has evaluated the rival interpretations of nature and found the scientific one to be the most intellectually satisfying. Instead of conquering the modern world first by proofs and demonstrations of practical value, modern science won by the attractiveness of its grasp of reality and its appeal to the ideals of modern humanity.

At this point, Polanyi has made the essential connection between science and freedom. The dangers of a philosophy that tries to eliminate all traditional beliefs and to base our knowledge only upon the testimony of the senses become apparent. Such a philosophy will eventually undermine science itself as well as the foundations of a free society.

Such is the main argument of Polanyi's first systematic philosophical statement. Following the way science makes discoveries, he placed the issue of scientific objectivism in a larger context which opens up the need to rethink our basic conception of scientific knowledge. This more comprehensive view is the beginning of his new theory of knowledge. As Polanyi's work continues, it becomes more apparent that unless there is a general epistemological reform, the goals and the institutions of a free and humane society are in jeopardy. This theory of knowledge becomes the problem and task of Michael Polanyi as he continues his quest for understanding our plight and its solutions.

TOWARDS A POST-CRITICAL PHILOSOPHY

The opportunity to develop his thought into a theory of knowledge came with two events. One was the exchanging of his chair in physical chemistry for a professorial appointment in social thought, free of lecturing duties. He now was able to devote himself full time to philosophical studies. The second event was the invitation to give the Gifford Lectures at the University of Aberdeen in 1951–52. These lectures may well mark a watershed in the history of philosophy. After a vast and thorough inquiry into the nature of knowledge, its origins, and its implications for current epistemology, Polanyi sets forth a challenging proposal for a post-critical philosophy. Three hundred and twenty-five years after Descartes began the skeptical tradition of modern philosophy, Polanyi, with his theory of personal knowledge, puts paid to this critical search for certainty.

Six years after the Gifford Lectures, Polanyi published his theory as *Personal Knowledge: Towards a Post-Critical Philosophy*. It is his magnum opus. Working from the Gifford Lectures, he has increased the range of evidence and of argument into a truly alternative ideal of knowledge. What he intends is not a mere correction nor caution concerning the personal element of knowledge. He aims for a general reform. It would be a serious misunderstanding to think that he is trying to point up the limitations and dangers in our knowledge arising from our personal bias. His aim is virtually the opposite. He seeks to show that the personal co-efficients of knowledge functioning through a structure of tacit activities are the most dominant and essential part. The personal is

[47]

not a hindering factor but the intelligent center of knowledge. The importance of considering knowledge from the angle of discovery is that it makes this point most clear.

The preface to *Personal Knowledge* summarizes elegantly the aim and nature of Polanyi's theory of knowledge. It reads like a manifesto, and because of its clarity and incisiveness is given here. He first states the goal and range of his work:

This is primarily an enquiry into the nature and justification of scientific knowledge. But my reconsideration of scientific knowledge leads on to a wide range of questions outside science.

I start by rejecting the ideal of scientific detachment. In the exact sciences, this false ideal is perhaps harmless, for it is in fact disregarded there by scientists. But we shall see that it exercises a destructive influence in biology, psychology, and sociology, and falsifies our whole outlook far beyond the domain of science. I want to establish an alternative ideal of knowledge quite generally.

Hence the wide scope of this book and hence also the coining of the new term I have used for my title: Personal Knowledge. *The two words may seem to contradict each other: for true knowledge is deemed impersonal, universally established, objective. But the seeming contradiction is resolved by modifying the conception of knowing.*

Next Polanyi gives an account of his conception of the way we achieve our knowledge:

I have used the findings of Gestalt psychology as my first clues to this conceptual reform. Scientists have run away from the philosophical implications of Gestalt; I want to countenance them uncompromisingly. I regard knowing as an active comprehension of the things known, an action that requires skill. Skilful knowing and doing is performed by subordinating a set of particulars, as clues or tools, to the shaping of a skilful achievement, whether

[48]

practical or theoretical. We may then be said to become "subsidiarily aware" of these particulars within our "focal awareness" of the coherent entity that we achieve. Clues and tools are things used as such and not observed in themselves. They are made to function as extensions of our bodily equipment and this involves a certain change of our own being. Acts of comprehension are to this extent irreversible, and also non-critical. For we cannot possess any fixed framework within which the re-shaping of our hitherto fixed framework could be critically tested.

Then Polanyi points out the significance of this new conception of knowledge:

Such is the personal participation *of the knower in all acts of understanding. But this does not make our understanding* subjective. *Comprehension is neither an arbitrary act nor a passive experience, but a responsible act claiming universal validity. Such knowing is indeed* objective *in the sense of establishing contact with a hidden reality; a contact that is defined as the condition for anticipating an indeterminate range of yet unknown (and perhaps yet inconceivable) true implications. It seems reasonable to describe this fusion of the personal and the objective as Personal Knowledge.*

Finally Polanyi states that all knowledge is fiduciary in character and consequently so are all the affirmations of his work:

Personal knowledge is an intellectual commitment, and as such inherently hazardous. Only affirmations that could be false can be said to convey objective knowledge of this kind. All affirmations published in this book are my own personal commitments; they claim this, and no more than this, for themselves.
Throughout this book I have tried to make this situation apparent. I have shown that into every act of knowing there enters a passionate contribution of the person knowing what is being known, and that this coefficient is no mere imperfection but a vital component

[49]

of his knowledge. And around this central fact I have tried to construct a system of correlative beliefs which I can sincerely hold, and to which I can see no acceptable alternatives. But ultimately, it is my own allegiance that upholds these convictions, and it is on such warrant alone that they can lay claim to the reader's attention.[23]

In the acknowledgment of our personal responsibility for all of our knowledge and in the recognition of the adventure that knowing involves, Polanyi's invitation to a Society of Explorers has begun.

Personal Knowledge is organized into four parts moving from specific inquiries in the most exact sciences toward larger investigations of articulate intelligence and ending in a general theory of knowledge. Part One, "The Art of Knowing," is demonstrative and indicative. It looks at scientific knowledge by examining objectivity in cases of scientific discovery in physics and chemistry and in conceptions of probability and of order. Even in these most exact areas of science, Polanyi finds scientific judgment to depend essentially upon personal coefficients that are tacit and exercised as skills. Rather than the objectivist picture of an impersonal calculation and reading of computations, he sees that formulas and rules are used like tools. Success depends not only upon precision but also upon the knack and art of the user.

Part Two, "The Tacit Component," is analytical. It uncovers the roots of the tacit coefficients of our personal knowledge. Drawing upon evidence in animal psychology, linguistics, learning-theory, sociology of knowledge, and mathematics he finds that all our formalized expressions are extensions of prearticulate components of intelligence. Intelligence, whether shown in works of art, mathematics, or ordinary conversations, is a development of faculties that are prelinguistic in origin and guided by personal and social satisfactions that are also only semiarticulate, such as the satisfactions of beauty or of sharing. The tacit components of our articulate intelligence appear then to be the larger domain and foundation upon which knowledge is built. A fallacy of the objective ideal is its identifying knowledge with what can be made explicit.

In Part Three, "The Justification of Personal Knowledge," the evidence of the first two sections is synthesized into a program of epistemological reform. Consideration is given to the views of contemporary British philosophy, automation and cybernation, and religious beliefs as they bear upon the fact of the tacit component in all knowing. The inescapable hazards of seeking to know with universal intent are accepted as the condition and calling of our human nature.

The final part of the book, "Knowing and Being," shows the place of personal knowledge in understanding living beings, including the knowledge of our own existence and the existence of other living persons. Here the relation between the theory of personal knowledge and the nature of reality is amplified. The structure of our knowing turns out to be a reflection of the structure of being. The way the explicit elements of our knowing rely upon the tacit elements in order to achieve integration and meaning points to the way hierarchy in evolution functions to produce conscious persons.

With *Personal Knowledge*, Polanyi established himself as a major and creative philosopher of this century. From this point of understanding, he continued his efforts in investigating and extending the philosophy that he had begun. He first showed that a post-critical philosophy meant a revision in our ways of understanding human nature. In *The Study of Man*, Polanyi applied his theory to the relations of the natural sciences, social sciences, and humanities and claimed a continuity and common ground for their knowledge.[24] Numerous lectureships and distinguished visiting professorships encouraged the sharing and refinement of his ideas.[25] Although his acclaim shows a greater interest in him by American scholars, Polanyi was, from 1960 on, a Senior Research Fellow at Merton College, Oxford. While Oxford philosophy persisted in its emphasis upon lucidity through analytical and linguistic philosophy, Polanyi published *The Tacit Dimension* in 1966 challenging these very assumptions.

The Tacit Dimension plays an important role in the totality of Polanyi's thought. Based upon the Yale, Duke, and Wesleyan lectures, the work sets forth Polanyi's epistemology in an economical yet comprehensive statement. In many ways it is the theoretical formulation of the work achieved in *Personal Knowledge* and *The Study of Man,* but it is also a development in evidence, argument, and clarity. Its shortcoming as an introduction to Polanyi's thought is that its brevity precludes the scope of evidence and analysis given in *Personal Knowledge.* The reader of only *The Tacit Dimension* is barely given a glimpse of the enormous evidence and research that led to this theory. It is doubtful that one can grasp the significance of Polanyi's theory without also weighing the arguments of *Personal Knowledge.*

The commanding importance of Polanyi's philosophy is brought to a culmination in his last major work, entitled *Meaning.*[26] Completed with the assistance of Professor Harry Prosch, *Meaning* demonstrates the profundity of Polanyi's heuristic theory of knowledge as a general theory for our culture. Moving from the nature of discovery and the critique of objectivism, Polanyi traces the role of tacit knowing in the creative imagination that works in literature, painting, myth, and religion. In ways never stated before in his philosophy, Polanyi shows how meaning is structured by the way we attend to the natural in science and to the transnatural in the humanities. Through these additional concepts, Polanyi is able to clarify further how tacit knowing functions in all of our knowing and yet how there is a distinctive way in which the imagination works in science and in the arts, as we shall see in Chapter IV.

Published only a few months before his death on February 22, 1976, *Meaning* rounds out Polanyi's philosophical mission to restore respect for the pursuit of truth and for the conditions of a free society conducive to it. It is Polanyi's aim that his view of the foundations of knowing will again renew the meaningfulness of traditional human ideals that were undercut by the scientific outlook and will enable humans to have a responsible place in the universe.

Our survey here of Polanyi's move from science to philosophy only introduces the background and breadth of his thought. We have neglected the more than one hundred papers in social and philosophical thought, his involvement with the Congress for Cultural Freedom, and the conferences generated by his ideas. But from this outline, we are better prepared to consider his alternative to the scientific outlook and the objective ideal of knowledge.

iii. A New Paradigm

A BASIC CHANGE

The significance of Michael Polanyi's philosophy can best be described as a new paradigm.[1] A paradigm expresses the configuration of beliefs, values, and techniques by which normal science is pursued. It represents the outlook and methods by which a discipline of study conducts its routine life, interprets data, and does research. A paradigm provides metaphors, analogies, explanations, and standards for solutions to puzzles. Paradigms are adopted because they both win adherence of followers and are sufficiently open-ended to allow focus upon further research. The breakdown of old paradigms and the emergence of new ones is a case of major revolution, usually involving preceding periods of crisis and the search for new directions. The establishment of new paradigms is a moment of synthesis and of originality. The contradictions and the clues from the earlier paradigm period and its stages of disintegration are assembled into a new orientation that continues and renews the field, yet it is a decidedly different situation, for all things are seen from a totally new perspective. One of the foremost examples is the paradigm change in connection with the change from a geocentric to a heliocentric view of planetary motion. This change in perspective meant a sweeping revision of our ideas, from the place of humanity in the scheme of things to the nature of motion itself. Only by seeing Polanyi's philosophy on this scale can we see what he means by "a post-critical philosophy."

The change sought by Polanyi's theory of knowledge is like the paradigm changes that have entailed scientific revolutions. Science has taught itself in the paradigm of knowledge believed to be derived from the sixteenth- and seventeenth-century scientific revolution in astronomy, physics, and mathematics. This paradigm is a generalization that is now discovered to be only partly true and greatly contradictory. It attempted to establish knowledge with certainty independent of the person and to gain the precision and mechanical character of Newton's laws. As much as Copernicus changed the former world view by making the earth revolve around the sun, Polanyi is changing it by making all knowledge revolve around the responsible person. The old paradigm was based upon a separation of logic and psychology. It tried to understand the nature of inference and reasoning without including the central role of the whole person.

Not only are there parallels between the level and power of Polanyi's thought and the making of other paradigm changes, but there are also parallels in the historical events involved. Polanyi's discovery of tacit knowing is the development of a potentiality recognized since the time of Plato at least. Major philosophers have noticed what Polanyi calls the tacit dimension. As in the story of other creative innovations in thought, it is the concurrence of events in our time that has brought together the elements necessary for a gifted mind to bring this new theory to light. To present Polanyi's philosophy as the articulation of a new paradigm is a bold assertion. We are only at the beginning of a new era in thought, and it is difficult to stand in the midst of a stream with changing currents and convince others of the best course. It was 144 years from Copernicus's *De Revolutionibus* (1543) to Newton's *Principia Mathematica* (1687) which gave final confirmation of Copernicus's theory. Great as this achievement was, it was not until 1948 that the description "scientific revolution" came into common usage to characterize this period.[2] Yet in our period of rapid change and increased knowledge of events on a global scale, combined with a sense of history, we may be able to discern the general direction of our future. At least, we are contending here that Polanyi's epistemology is the formulation of a new paradigm that opens up the needed new direction for human progress in the period ahead. Whether or not this alternative will be accepted and lead to the necessary changes in our world views cannot be foretold. Too many contingencies are involved. At this juncture, we can try to see what Polanyi's alternative is and how it is the inauguration of a new paradigm.

A NEW VIEW OF KNOWING

To see Polanyi's thought as a new paradigm, we shall have to put ourselves into a new framework in order to understand it. We shall need for the moment to be willing to suspend old habits of thought and to try to entertain the vision that he has given. We shall make a pastiche out of his theory borrowing freely from his many works and constructing an imaginary story that illustrates the role of the tacit dimension in fundamental cases of knowing.

Let us suppose that one night as we are asleep in our bed we are suddenly awakened by a noise. Within seconds we are wide awake, alert, listening attentively. We ask: "Is it the wind? A burglar? A rat?. . . We try to guess. Was that a footfall? That means a burglar! Convinced we pluck up courage, rise, and proceed to verify our assumption."[3] Quietly we descend the stairs where it is dark and turn toward the kitchen where a light is seen filtering under the foot of the door. As we enter, a man is filling a bag with small

[57]

appliances and the family silver. Surprised by our arrival, the burglar turns and leaps forward trying to leave by the door. We bar it with our body; a struggle ensues. All at once the lights seem to go out. It is moments later when we regain consciousness. Our stomach is wet, covered with blood. The police need to be notified; a doctor is needed. But no one else is there. We have no telephone and no car. Slowly we manage to stand up and to stagger to the porch, climb on our bicycle, and pedal cautiously to the village hospital.[4]

The next time we awaken we are in a clean and busy hospital room. We feel a pain in our side and reaching, find we are swathed in bandages. The doctor comes in and tells us that we had a bad knife wound.[5] It took fifteen stitches to close it. No serious internal damage though. Next the police enter and ask for details of the assault and robbery. They ask if we know the person or have ever seen him before. Since we do not know the assailant, they bring in pictures and we begin to try to identify him.[6]

The incident creates a temporary stir in the village. Reporters come, and there are stories in the newspapers. We lie in bed recovering and slightly enjoy the publicity and the reading about ourself in the evening newspaper.[7] One day we get a letter that is in French.[8] We read it and beam with comfort from the attention that our mishap is getting. The nurse enters and says that we are looking well. It's nearly time for us to go home. We tell her about our dear friend who has just written from Paris.

In the course of this brief and simple story, we have engaged in a number of intelligent activities, and they all illuminate the nature of knowing. Drawn from Polanyi's various illustrations we have seen: 1) the recognizing of a problem and the determination of a solution: "There's a burglar in the house!" 2) a skillful performance: riding a bicycle with a serious wound, 3) a skillful diagnosis and use of tools: the medical doctor's operation, 4) the recognition of a physiognomy: the police method of identification, and 5) the reading of a text: the newspaper reports and a letter in a foreign language. Analysis of these feats of knowledge will help us to begin to see what Polanyi means.

[58]

Retracing our story, we notice first that Polanyi sees a parallel between the discovery of a burglar and the art of guessing right in science. Scientific discovery has to work with clues that could mean many different things. The success of science is in its training to pay attention to clues that are important. Yet this attention is a complex matter, for it involves the integration of seemingly random data into a meaningful pattern. One point then is to look for light on this crucial function; integrating clues into meaningful knowledge.

Turning to the next part of the story, our amazing bicycle ride to the hospital, we recognize skills. Bicycle riding is a complex matter, if you have ever tried to learn by reading a book about it or tried to explain it to someone wanting to learn. Details, explicit instructions, and even demonstrations do not work easily. The rider also has to integrate a large number of factors. Most people do this satisfactorily, but it is a skillful performance which they cannot explain nor can they easily do with only a set of written instructions.

The work of the doctor is a striking case. Through his knowledge, he has to perform the difficult task of visualizing our interior anatomy and of probing into it with instruments so that he understands the proper functioning of our organs. We are appropriately awed by the skill that extends itself through surgical tools inside the labyrinth of our bodies and aids them. Polanyi observes that here we have a very dramatic form of the integration of clues, for the intelligence of the doctor is carried from his mind into the tissues of our body. The integration of clues by the doctor is not only intelligent but it is also an indwelling as his skill touches our interior organs so dexterously.

The identification of a physiognomy is a classic example of tacit knowing. We have in descriptive science the same principle at work. The ability to identify the burglar who robbed and attacked us is akin to the recognition of a coherent pattern among clues in nature. Modern police methods have developed an array of facial features—noses, eyes, ears, mouths—that a witness may assemble into a likeness of the suspect. The remarkable thing is that the witness already has these clues in his or her memory but cannot fully tell them to someone else. The police method facilitates the integration of clues, but it requires the witness's intelligent cooperation.

The reading of a text is another form of knowing so common that we scarcely notice its complexity. Polanyi observes here how we perform many feats of integration without being aware that we are doing them. For example, we get the meaning of a sentence or a whole story without concentrating upon grammar, syntax, and vocabulary. These parts of our knowledge are definitely a part of any intelligent reading. When we read, we place these things at the service of our purpose of getting the meaning, and we do not think "subject," "predicate," "tense," and so on. If we did, it would lead to something else, and we would temporarily lose our meaning. The reading of a letter in French and then conveying its meaning in English to the nurse shows how easily we attain meaning by attending to the joint meaning of clues rather than their details in themselves. When we tell someone about the contents of a letter in French, we do not think about the French itself but the meaning of what was said. As Polanyi says, such an experience is like that of the person who discovered he had been speaking prose all of his life.

If our introduction to the paradigm that Polanyi is articulating has been successful, we shall have begun to grasp that knowing is a type of tacit integration of clues into meaning. Furthermore, we may have seen enough instances to gather that all knowing, from practical routine tasks to highly skillful theoretical feats, shares in this process of integration. Whether we are reading dials, pondering computer printouts, tracing isotopes, or building theoretical models, we are making a movement from clues or particulars to wholes. Our interest is so much upon what these particulars mean together that we usually do not even notice them directly. If we do stop to concentrate on them individually, this shift of attention will also change what we are doing, as we lose sight temporarily of the total task or problem. If, for example, in identifying a physiognomy we concentrate upon a blemish on the nose, we lose the image of the whole face momentarily. But through this type of analysis or emphasis upon detail, we may gain some advantage and be able to say to the police, "Look for a man with a scar on his face." Still any further identification will depend upon a renewed integration of all the details into the characteristic physiognomy.

The thrust of Polanyi's emphasis upon tacit integration is to carry us into looking at a new structure for understanding knowing. Clearly, such acts of understanding as we have just seen highly involve the person in the achievement of knowledge. Inferences from isolated or randomly-given clues will not provide knowledge and meaning. Someone has to find their joint significance. By continuing into Polanyi's theory at a slightly more technical level, we can see how Gestalt psychology provided the key to how science makes discoveries and led to Polanyi's new theory.

THE CLUE FROM GESTALT PSYCHOLOGY

One of the earliest known references by Polanyi to Gestalt psychology occurs in an article in 1941 on "The Growth of Thought in Society."[9] Here he is still struggling with the freedom of science, and he draws upon the ideas of Gestalt to argue for decentralized control. He contends that there is more than one form of order besides a predetermined one given by centralized scientific planning. From the work of Wolfgang Köhler in Gestalt psychology, Polanyi shows that there can be order of the highest complexity spontaneously achieved by internal mutual adjustment. This interest in Gestalt findings in relation to creative intellectual endeavor became the foundation of a major new insight.

Gestalt psychology demonstrates the way we perform the five tacit integrations that we have just surveyed. In the above examples, we saw that we had a knowledge that we could not completely tell. There was what Polanyi calls "the tacit dimension." We could not explain the successful leap from "noises" to "a burglar in the house" without relying upon our art of guessing. We could not explain the angle, the velocity, and the force of bicycle riding, yet we did it effectively without a detailed knowledge of the principles of physics. We put clues together in the reading of a text, the identifying of the assailant, and the performing of a difficult operation. In each case, there was this unexplained dimension, the jump from particulars to a meaningful whole.

Gestalt provided the clue to how we perform these acts of tacit integration. According to the theory of Gestalt psychology, we know the coherence or pattern of an object by a spontaneous equilibration of visual clues or stimuli that are impressed on the retina or the brain.[10] We are unaware of the particulars or clues themselves, but we know them in the object that we recognize or the activity that we do. In this suggestion, Polanyi saw a significant implication that was undeveloped by Gestalt psychology itself. Speaking of "spontaneous equilibrations of visual clues," Gestalt psychology shied away from acknowledgment of the active involvement of the person in knowing. Instead of avoiding this conclusion, Polanyi drew it forcefully. In his words:

However, I am looking at Gestalt, on the contrary, as the outcome of an active shaping of experience performed in the pursuit of knowledge. This shaping or integrating I hold to be the great and indispensable tacit power by which all knowledge is discovered and, once discovered, is held to be true.[11]

From this insight, Polanyi began to collect evidence and to develop his theory of knowledge in its most precise form.

To continue our pursuit of the depth of the new paradigm and its content, we have to move to more sophisticated data. One example is Polanyi's treatment of two experiments in subception.[12] These experiments illuminate the dynamics of knowing by calling our attention to the feat of doing something intelligently without being able to tell how we did it, and they reveal a from-to structure that is involved. Lazarus and McCleary in 1949 showed that a person who was presented rapidly with a large number of nonsense syllables, in which certain syllables were followed by an electric shock, could learn to anticipate the shock syllables; yet, on being questioned the subject could not tell what the shock syllables were. A similar experiment was reported in 1958 by Eriksen and Kuethe. Here the subject was administered a shock whenever he uttered anything associated with certain words. Again, the questioning of the subject disclosed that he did not know that he had learned to identify the shock words and to avoid them. Both cases represent instances of tacit knowing.

In analyzing these examples, Polanyi observes how the person integrates what seem to be two distinct elements into a form of knowledge. One element is the experimental subject's consciousness of the electrical shock. This element can be explicitly denoted. The subject can say that he feels an electrical shock. This sensation, to a certain extent, holds his attention. This element is what the subject is "attending to." A second element is also present, namely, the subceived syllables. These subceptions contain the pattern in which the electrical shocks occur. In order to deal with the electrical shock itself, the subject has "to rely upon" this experienced but undefined pattern. Whenever the subject learns to anticipate the shocks or to suppress the associations that trigger them, he has integrated these two parts into a form of knowledge.

These experiments in subception yield an important explanation. They help us to see why all knowledge is an act of tacit knowing. Looking at these experiments, we see a number of things. First is that the concern of the subject is focused upon the electrical shock itself. His aim is to deal with the shock irritations. This attention explains why the shock-producing syllables remain tacit in his awareness. His knowledge of these particulars is only through their bearing on the electrical shock. Second, we see that the shock-producing syllables are tacitly known in connection with the electrical shock. The experimental subject has a "subsidiary awareness" but not a "focal awareness" of the syllables.

Here then is the fundamental structure of all knowing. It is really "a triad," for three centers of knowing are involved.[13] First, we have a focal target. Sometimes we might call it a problem. Our efforts are directed to this point. Second, we have clues of which we are only subsidiarily aware. Sometimes we can stop to pinpoint some of them, but at other times we cannot. We might say, "I know that these nonsense syllables have something to do with this." Or we might say, "The sounds we hear suggest a burglar in the house." When these clues have meaning, they function as a part of something other than themselves alone. They become part of our knowing how to deal with the shocks or of our formulation of the burglar hypothesis. In this way, we rely upon the clues subsidiarily for attending to something else. Finally, we have the person who links our focal target with our subsidiary clues. This third center of knowing is crucial to our recognition of the change in paradigm that Polanyi's analysis entails. The operations in which we move from our clues to their joint meaning are an achievement of the person. It is a process of inference. It is a process done within our body. And it is one that cannot be focally observed by us. We cannot simultaneously rely upon clues for attending to a problem or task and observe them in themselves. In this sense, there will always be a tacit dimension in our knowledge that is held together by the person.

Much more is to be unfolded about the nature of the structure of knowing, but it is valuable now to refer to our larger problem of the objective ideal of knowledge. The structure of tacit knowing shows that the objective ideal is mistakenly preoccupied with only a fraction of what is involved. Formulas, measurements, and topographies cannot be read without subsidiary awareness. Theories or laws cannot be perceived without tacit integration of data and ideas into wholes. Even smells, colors, tastes, and a thousand other seemingly insignificant clues and suggestions enter into our solutions. This triadic structure upon which we rely can readily be discerned once it is called to our attention, yet we have difficulty fathoming its weighty implications after centuries of believing in the objective ideal. We can perhaps begin to see that the objective ideal of knowledge omits two major areas of knowing, our subsidiary reliance upon clues and our integrative powers as persons.

NEW TERMS

A new theory of knowledge of revolutionary proportions demands a vocabulary with which to express its meaning. In order to take up the newness of its themes, it has to formulate new terms that will signify the meaning that has been found. At the same time, the terminology has to be cast into the order of the theory itself and must show the adequacy and coherence of the theory. It is particularly the achievement of Polanyi since the publication of *Personal Knowledge* that he has met these needs of his epistemology with further developments. As a way of holding these technical elaborations of his work together, we shall again use an imaginative device.

Our setting is a museum of art. On display in a small room is a series of six woodblock prints done in a modern style. Because of their semirealistic character, it will take some effort to understand them. Each one is based upon an element of Polanyi's epistemology. As we grasp the meaning of the text under each print and its connection with the design of the picture, we shall ourselves have to perform the integrative feat of tacit knowing. In the course of this exhibition, a change may occur in our understanding. Once we have solved the puzzle of the meaning of these pictures, we shall find that our achievement is irreversible. We shall not be able to look at them again in the same puzzled way that we did at first. This experience of learning is another evidence of the reality of our tacit powers. For the meaning of the pictures is not strictly objective. It is something that we participate in, and once we participate, we interiorize clues and form integrations that remain with us to various degrees.[14]

Our first picture is labeled with Polanyi's aphorism about the tacit dimension, "We know more than we can tell."[15]

The drawing represents the artist's version of an iceberg, indicating the presence of a hidden dimension. What we have been accustomed to call knowledge is like the peak of the iceberg, and we have neglected‚ the greater part of knowledge itself because it is hidden from our direct view when we are using it. Like the bottom

We know more
than we can tell

Figure 1. The Tacit Dimension

[66]

of the iceberg, the tacit dimension is always there, and a true account will have to acknowledge it.

The second picture bears the statement, "We know by relying on (subsidiary awareness) and by attending to (focal awareness)."[16] Here the artist chose the dramatic stance of a workman on a scaffolding high up in a modern skyscraper. Down below, cars and trees appear as little blocks and dots. The drawing is apt for the structure of tacit knowing. The inherent danger of the situation suggests the hazard that is involved in all of our knowledge. Like the workman, we have to take the risk of trusting the clues that have been given to us in order to have knowledge. There is no way to avoid this risk; we can only try to act responsibly with universal intent.

Another feature of the drawing is the emphasis upon structure itself. There are two awarenesses that are integrated by the workman. They represent two of three descriptive categories in Polanyi's thought. Two are already stated, namely, that all knowing is "a relying on" in order "to attend to" our task, meaning, or problem. These two types of awareness have been signified as "subsidiary awareness" and as "focal awareness." Polanyi adds to them a third descriptive category to catch the positional character of these two awarenesses. That to which we are attending seems to be at a distance from us. Hence, he calls the focal awareness the "distal term." Yet the things upon which we rely are close; they are interiorized. While we are relying upon them, we cannot focus upon them without changing our performance or our awareness. The subsidiary awareness is therefore called the "proximal term."[17] These refinements may appear unnecessary at first. But in a complex discussion of epistemology, they become valuable as they indicate the active, the functional, and the positional character of the elements of knowing, helping to show that meaning cannot be dichotomized between the object and the knower nor reduced merely to the object.

Our next four pictures deal with well-known events and problems. The one we see first is based on an ancient discovery. It depicts a crown and a man bathing.

we know by relying on
(subsidiary awareness)
and by attending to
(focal awareness)

Figure 2. Two Types of Awareness

subsidiary awareness
functions to guide us
to the integration of a
coherent pattern

Figure 3. Indwelling

[69]

According to history, Archimedes was asked to determine if the king's crown was made of pure gold or if it was mixed with baser metals. Since the crown was of irregular shape, it was difficult to measure and to compare its volume with an equal volume of gold. One day Archimedes climbed into his bath, and as the water rose through the displacement by his body, he is reputed to have exclaimed, "Eureka!" Focally aware of the problem of weighing the king's crown after days of worrying over it, and also subsidiarily aware of the rise of the water, he linked the two terms into the principle that bears his name. The story of Archimedes' finding the principle of displacement of liquids is especially relevant to the text, "Subsidiary awareness functions to guide us to the integration of a coherent pattern."[18] Archimedes' discovery exemplifies the fact that scientific discovery proceeds through tacit knowing. The intuitive flash springs from our subsidiary awareness which has served to orient us toward new understanding.[19]

This picture may also be used to underline another element of tacit knowing, the element of indwelling.[20] As Archimedes used his bodily experience to guide him to a major discovery, we can see that the nature of tacit knowing means that our body is the instrument by which we know the world. The structure of tacit knowing explains how we use our body to attend from it to things outside of it. When we rely upon clues, we interiorize and dwell in them as the proximal terms of our existence. That our knowing is always a form of indwelling is one of the revolutionary aspects of Polanyi's theory leading to a new paradigm. It overthrows centuries of dichotomies that have separated mind and body, reason and experience, subject and object, the knower and the known.

We still have three more pictures in our exhibition, but before we proceed there is a major feature of the whole display that needs to be called to our attention. So far, we have seen illustrations of the structure of tacit knowing and of how the subsidiary and focal elements are united into an intelligible pattern. Some opponents of Polanyi's view might feel that they could concur without danger to their views with what we have presented. They might be willing to grant that there is a tacit dimension or a knowledge that we know and cannot tell, but they would argue that this analysis belongs to psychology, and the important part of epistemology belongs to the explicit domain. Nothing could be more wrong.[21] Polanyi is asserting that the processes of inference, wherever they occur, entail a relying upon subsidiary awareness in order to attend to tasks, problems, or meaning focally. Moreover, it is this very process of tacit knowing that functions to guide us to any knowledge at all. Tacit knowing is not just a psychological precondition or background, but it is an integral part of the logic of knowing. Our example from Archimedes suggests this fact, but the next three exhibits will make it more emphatic.

The text of the fourth picture, "Subsidiary particulars appear in the phenomenon of the pattern they produce," is one way of showing how the form of integration is constantly rooted in tacit knowing. If this picture could have sound effects, the stage directions would be, "Absolute silence!"

One of the major developments of the last two decades is a public ecological awareness. The writing of Rachel Carson contributed strongly to the sense of alarm over the use of pesticides. In her book *Silent Spring* Carson tells how she began to notice one springtime that the chorus of birds usually heard was becoming inaudible. She asked herself what had happened and began the investigation that led to her controversial work. For our purposes, the story is a useful one because it shows one of the ways that the subsidiary particulars become a part of knowledge: they appear in the knowledge itself. Polanyi calls this "the phenomenal structure" of knowing.[22] The actual hush that Carson experienced in her subsidiary awareness appeared in the pattern of a silent spring, a pattern whose exploration led to important concerns. The artist's picture points to the ultimate implication of a world without birds by suggesting that our destruction of living things in the life chain can mean our own death. Clearly, whenever we form an integration or recognize a shape or pattern in nature, we are beholding the phenomenon of subsidiary particulars in their joint appearance.

Our fifth picture shows a discrimination between the appearance of pattern and the meaning of pattern which underlines again

[71]

Subsidiary particulars
appear in the phenomenon
of the pattern they produce

Figure 4. Phenomenal Aspect

[72]

Subsidiary particulars
and awareness bear
on what they mean

Figure 5. Semantic Aspect

[73]

the distinctive contribution of the individual in all knowing. Different persons may perceive the same pattern without finding the same meaning. Yet in the achievement of meaning, we also rely upon the subsidiary awareness of the proximal clues. The picture continues the ecological motif by alluding to the title of another popular book.

When Paul Ehrlich wrote *The Population Bomb,* he drew a frightening connection between the geometric acceleration of population growth and the ecological dangers to our world. In Polanyi's language, we could say that Ehrlich gave a meaning to the phenomenon of silent springtimes. The pattern of silence bore a dire signal. In this way our integration of clues into a pattern that gives meaning shows "the semantic aspect" of knowing that depends upon the tacit dimension.[23]

In isolating the semantic aspect of knowing in this way, Polanyi also brings to our attention the strength of his theory and the weakness of the prevailing theories of explicit knowledge. Meaning lies in the distal term or terms. This area is the one that we are usually studying. The meaningfulness of the distal term depends, however, upon the proximal clues upon which it relies. Meaning cannot exist by itself. It requires a person who can integrate clues into coherent patterns that he or she can see as meaningful. Neither is meaning arbitrary. It belongs to a structure of comprehending relationships such as we have seen, and this takes us to the last figure of the exhibit.

Here the artist places before us an image of one of the most vivid metaphors of the ecological movement. The text, "Tacit knowing guides us to comprehension of something real," indicates that our integrations are toward things that are universal.

In this drawing, we see a globe that has a mechanical structure. The globe is floating in air. Beneath the globe are forms suggestive of the wings sometimes seen in aerodynamics illustrations. The intent of this flying orb with its lonely feeling is to capture the sense of Barbara Ward's description of the human situation today as "spaceship earth." The shrinking of the world through our increased interdependence has given us both the intimacy and the

Tacit knowing guides
us to comprehension
of something real

Figure 6. Ontological Aspect

[75]

precariousness of a spaceship. It has also given us the opportunity and responsibility of learning to work together to keep the spaceship aloft. From this perspective, we can grasp that the tacit feats of knowing lead not only to pattern (silent spring) and to meaning (population explosion) but also to reality (ecological interdependence). The sum of the clues about ecology is to guide us toward a deeper truth about the structure of our existence. The pattern and meaning that we confront are ways of our discovering new features of reality. This connecting of proximal terms with distal terms so that new horizons are opened to us Polanyi calls "the ontological aspect" of tacit knowing.[24] The significance of knowing is that it is not only about our own feelings or thoughts but about reality, too. Such a theory of knowing becomes a theory of responsibility. We are called upon to so live in the clues that are given us by tradition and inquiry that we can rely upon them to guide us to the inexhaustible features of reality.

This element of responsibility is present in the "universal intent" of our knowing.[25] In relying upon the clues given to us, we cannot strictly assure that we shall be right. Our knowing is a search for the truth through the matrix of our existence. The personal in us seeks to link the awareness within to the external reality beyond. We are not free to do as we please but called to respond to the clues and problems that can be ascertained by us and other competent persons. Our satisfaction is not in pleasing ourselves but in our contact with aspects of reality that can be found by others and offer prospect of further discovery.

With our "exhibition tour" and commentary completed, we can now step back to see all of this together. The following diagram attempts to show in summary the major terms and their roles in Polanyi's theory of knowledge.

Besides reviewing the technical terms of the theory, the diagram attempts to show the interlocking character of the various structures of knowledge by using the infinity symbol of a figure eight lying on its side instead of two separate circles for self and object.[26] In the nature of indwelling, subsidiary awareness and focal awareness are always interdependent and grow mutually in our know-

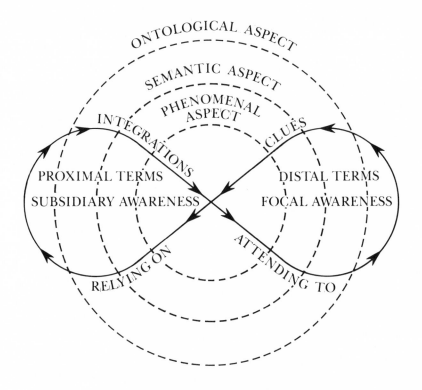

Diagram of Tacit Knowing

ledge. An increase in the explicit domain of knowledge also involves an increase in the tacit domain which, in turn enables us to increase our explicit knowledge again, and so on. The outside circles running through the infinity symbol serve to indicate that all aspects of our knowledge, from the appearance of pattern (phenomenal aspect) through the meaning of pattern (semantic aspect) to the bearing of pattern and meaning upon reality (onto-logical aspect), constantly depend upon the simultaneous and dynamic functioning of subsidiary and focal awareness. In this new paradigm, it is now clearer that knowledge is neither sub-jective nor objective but a transcendence of both achieved by the person acting with universal intent. Such then is both the hazard and the adventure of knowing, conditions that we are challenged to accept responsibly.

TACIT KNOWING AND CLASSIC PHILOSOPHY

Frequently the birth of a new paradigm comes from features and problems overlooked or discounted in previous periods. Later these features germinate, and at the right moment when new problems and dissatisfactions arise, they begin to show their potentiality. Polanyi often mentioned that Kant seemed to have acknowledged a tacit dimension in our knowledge, but Kant was unable to do anything constructive with the insight.[27] Instead Kant regarded this factor, which he called our "mother wit," as one so deeply hidden in our self that we were unlikely ever to understand its operations.

With the development of Polanyi's philosophy, some philosophers are beginning to observe that tacit knowing has a significant place in the history of philosophy.[28] One of the most convincing discussions of the place of tacit knowing in classic philosophy shows that Plato, Aristotle, and Hume all allowed for a tacit dimension in their thought, even though they did not emphasize or develop it.[29]

Beginning with Plato, it has been shown that his conception of knowledge inherently relies upon principles similar to those of tacit knowing.[30] Plato did not think that the Forms or Ideas which give us true knowledge could ever be made fully explicit. The knowledge of the Forms or Ideas is what is intended by our linguistic formulations, but Plato kept a distinction between these formulations and true knowledge itself. "Knowledge therefore does not exist in the form of our various explicit formulations, expressions, constructions or operations. It exists only in our *minds."* The exercise of dialectic or philosophical investigation is done with the hope that we shall "see" the Form or "get" the Idea.

[78]

Knowledge for Plato then could be said to be personal, in that each person has to grasp it for himself or herself and to judge it as knowledge. There is no way that knowledge can be objectified. In this sense, Plato's Ideas "were always only tacitly grasped."

Aristotle also seems to have allowed for the tacit dimension but not to have developed it.[31] He tried to deal with the problem of how we achieve empirical knowledge through induction. Significantly, Aristotle recognized that knowledge gained through scientific investigation is different from that in logical demonstration. In order to grasp the relation between observed instances and the expectation that these would be found in all such instances, Aristotle posited the element of intuition. It is "intuitive reasoning" that perceives the basic premises of a scientific syllogism. Furthermore, Aristotle followed the same approach in his ethics where the rule for finding the mean between two extremes cannot be stated explicitly, but a person of practical wisdom knows it.

Even Hume, a major modern empiricist, had a tacit dimension in several aspects of his account of knowledge.[32] His work is usually taken to be an advocacy of the idea of explicit objectivity. But his own admission that the certainty of the ideas of resemblance, contrariety, and degrees of quality is "discoverable at first sight" and is more properly a matter of "intuition than demonstration" discloses the role of tacit knowing in his thought. More examples could be given from Hume and other major philosophers of the past, but the point is now sufficiently clear. Tacit knowing is not a fiction but a dimension necessarily allowed, though undeveloped, by other philosophers. Not until the objective ideal of knowledge triumphed did the importance of tacit knowing arise in philosophy.

TACIT KNOWING AND PHILOSOPHY OF SCIENCE

When we examine current philosophy of science, we find that there is also an anticipation of tacit knowing. The paradigm of scientific

[79]

objectivism has broken down, and various attempts at revision are under way. These changes indicate the possibility of an eventual change in world view once the new paradigm is established. Most glaring in the revisions now in process is their failure to draw the full implications of the changes that they are making into a recognition of the emergence of a new paradigm.

One area of change very close to Polanyi's heuristic emphasis is the growing admission that there is no exact scientific method leading to discoveries.[33] The inductive method, idealized through the writings of Bacon, Hume, and Mill as leading to an amassing of empirical facts upon which scientific conclusions can be built, has turned out to be misleading. Data require interpretation, and the seeing of pattern and relationship is not inherent in the appearance of the data itself. On the other hand, the deductive process of predicting scientific results from generalizations or theories turns out to be partially useful in testing theories and of no use at all in accounting for the genesis of scientific concepts and theories. Instead, there has to be a recognition of the essential role of the creative imagination.[34]

In this connection, the close relationship between experiment and interpretation is again being discovered. The positivist attempt to do science as mere reporting of the scientific facts has failed. N. R. Hanson has shown that all data are "theory-laden" and that there is no such thing as uninterpreted facts.[35] Whatever is regarded as fact represents the consensus of scientific opinion at that time. The facts of science arise out of the shared experience of the scientific community. Only those who participate in this community are able to observe the data and see scientific validity in their observations.

A third area of change follows from the growing understanding of the communal nature of science. The truth of scientific claims is a function of the scientific community's judgment. This judgment is regulated and shaped by a set of attitudes and of expectations that are in a process of growth and change. Verification means satisfying the standards of science as they are currently practiced, not some absolute criteria that are always true. Toulmin and Kuhn have shown that the patterns of intelligibility and regularity that guide science in its interpretation of observations are ones that change over a long period of time and that are not easily tested, if at all.[36]

It is not surprising then that the idea of strict scientific proof has also been modified. It is now widely recognized that no scientific theory can be easily proved to be true. Copi and Margenau have observed that a whole network of ideas is involved in a scientific theory.[37] It is impossible to test directly a theory through a crucial experiment because so many interlocking assumptions are involved. The history of science displays many examples such as belief in natural selection, where science has triumphed by proceeding upon limited evidence, or by ignoring negative results. Even the retreat to a model of the probability of verification does not escape the scientist's dependence upon a variety of criteria that influence his or her decision to accept or reject the evidence. The element of personal judgment shaped by the scientific enterprise at that moment must enter into the decision.

While these alterations and insights into scientific process foreshadow a change in paradigm, they are also accompanied by a new awareness of the relation between the physical and social sciences. As the mistaken view of objectivism has declined, it has become more apparent that the sharp distinctions that were formerly drawn between these two fields are now more a matter of degree. Each field is neither wholly objective nor subjective in its knowledge and methods.

Paradigm changes are rarely singular and more often are a part of a larger realization at work in the society itself. To this extent, there are signs of paradigm disintegration in the new attitude of some parts of the general public. The protest against science and technology manifests a recognition of the limits of science when it is understood as impersonal objective truth. The criticism is not directed against the benefits of the rationality of science but against the way scientific and technological progress seem to depersonalize and dehumanize us. This represents a growing awareness of the importance of the person and human values within scientific process. These signs have appeared distinctly in the human potential movement where experiments in encounter groups and sensitivity training have attempted to introduce a personal dimension into our existence in a scientific and technological culture. This phenomenon is also repeated in the counterculture's search for a more human identity away from urban technology and in the demands at universities by students for more individual attention. While these instances are interesting and many-faceted, they share a common theme: a reaction to the ideal of detachment and impersonality which was fostered by the scientific outlook. The intensity of their energies and their imaginations can be taken as a clue to the revolution in our thought now taking place.

Once this scale of thought is seen, it becomes clearer that in many ways the arguments are already over. The separation of the knower and the known is no longer convincing even though that separation is institutionalized in our habits of thought, our ideals, and our organization of life. Instead of arguing further for it, the task seems to be one of understanding the new paradigm that has emerged and beginning to live within it. It is at this juncture that the work of Polanyi is important to us. He is not the first to criticize scientific objectivism. He is the first to provide a comprehensive alternative commensurate with the problems that we face. It is in this sense that we turn now to the exploration of the new paradigm.

iv. A Heuristic Philosophy

THE POINT OF VIEW

What will be the final name for Polanyi's philosophy is too early to tell at the present. William Scott has referred to it as a "Gestalt philosophy" and shown its affinity with aspects of existential philosophy.[1] Polanyi has indirectly suggested a label with his description of his aim as a "post-critical philosophy." In both cases, it seems that the terms are less distinctive than Polanyi's work. He has gone much further than Gestalt psychology, and his work is more constructive than the negative contrast with the period of critical philosophy. "Tacit knowing" also lends itself to describing his thought since it speaks of his fundamental contribution to epistemology. However, it has the limitation of not speaking readily of the wholeness of Polanyi's derivations from this discovery and of leaving some with the original quandary about our explicit knowledge. Since Polanyi's thought is not a minor change in the field of epistemology, but a comprehensive and alternative ideal, it needs a denotation that gathers up its decisive characteristic and suggests the range of its implications. For the moment, until a better term emerges, I am proposing to call Polanyi's articulation of a new paradigm "a heuristic philosophy."

The term "heuristic" seems to bring together and to emphasize the distinctive contribution of Polanyi's point of view. "Heuristic" derives from the Greek, *heuriskein,* to find or discover. The nature of discovery is the root idea that illuminates and motivates Polanyi's philosophy. When we follow through Polanyi's analysis, we find that it is not only an end to the subject-object dichotomies of modern philosophy, not only a refutation of the objective ideal of knowledge, but also a new vision that beckons us toward a responsible society of explorers.

The heuristic thread runs throughout Polanyi's thought and is the element that leads to a new understanding of knowledge and of ourselves. Earlier we saw that discovery and exploration in science were the seminal clues that enabled Polanyi to unlock our epistemological predicament. The question of how science makes discoveries led to tacit knowing, then to a reform of our conception of knowledge itself. This starting point needs to be kept in mind as a way of holding the breadth of Polanyi's thought together and seeing the emergence of a new paradigm. Throughout his work, the theme of finding, discovering, growing, expanding, enriching is constant. It is present in his view of science and all the arts.[2] It is present in his conception of reality.[3] It is in his observation of the story of life from incandescent gases and interstellar dust to humans and their future.[4] Viewed in its totality, Polanyi's philosophy is one that is aimed primarily at the equipping and encouraging of humans in the unending task of pursuing meaning and truth.[5] This focus guides his concern for individual and social freedom, his concern for liberty and creativity of thought, his concern for tradition and society, and his concern for science, politics, economics, philosophy, art, and religion. He is a thinker, like other great leaders of thought, who sets before us the opportunity for unlimited exploration if we can learn to live with the infinite under the conditions of finite existence. Discovery and exploration seem to be the distinctive elements in epistemology that reveal the structure of tacit knowing, the hierarchical nature of matter and life, the proper function of our private and civic institutions, and the major questions of human purpose. Certainly discovery is not the all of life now, in the past, or in the future; life is manifold, with many interests and values. But discovery seems to be the crucial focus for putting knowing in perspective and recovering the way for an ongoing humanity, a humanity that is free to be creative. Continuing from our development of Polanyi's philosophy in the previous chapters, we need to try to encompass the fullness of his thought and the challenge it presents.

The heuristic thread begins to be found in the nature of scientific discovery and scientific knowledge. When we inquire into how science finds and holds its knowledge, the story turns out to be radically different from the one we have been taught. Contrary to finding knowledge according to the principles of the objective ideal, science finds it by a process in which our personal powers are tacitly involved at every stage. We can deepen our understanding of this point by looking once more into Polanyi's analysis of scientific discovery.

SCIENCE AND REALITY

Science is pursued for its bearing on reality, but reality is not explicitly definable. It is one of the paradoxes of our knowledge that we accept science because we think it gives a truer account of reality, yet this account could be false. Much modern philosophy of science has given up the notion of reality because of the difficulty in defining it.[6] Still, we accept the results of science as true even though we do not have strict proof that they are. The logic of our acceptance of scientific reality is not based upon its precision but upon our belief that it is more reasonable to accept scientific results than to doubt them.

[85]

The source of this acceptance of science is found in the story of modern science itself.[7] Copernicus discovered the heliocentric system through ideas that convinced him but convinced few others. His system was far more complicated than the Ptolemaic one, involved many *ad hoc* assumptions, had mechanical difficulties, and introduced staggering assumptions about the distance of the fixed stars. Yet, Copernicus held to his claim that his system had unique harmonies which proved it to be real even though he could only describe these harmonies in emotional passages. In his claim that his system was real, Copernicus believed that it would produce future manifestations of its truthfulness. These manifestations did appear later when astronomers, who accepted his claim, explored his system further. This example discloses two features of reality in a scientific discovery: (1) "It is to believe that it refers to no chance configuration of things, but to a persistent connection of certain features, a connection which, being real, will yet manifest itself in numberless ways, inexhaustibly," and (2) "It is to believe that it is there, existing independently of us, and that hence its consequences can never be fully predicted."[8]

We can understand this discovery of reality through science by seeing it first as an extension of the kind of power of perception that we have already seen in tacit knowing. Here, we have found how all of our knowing functions with two types of awareness, subsidiary and focal. Our explicit knowledge of anything is the achievement of a focal integration of subsidiary clues and stimuli on which we rely. Science is a way of seeing things in nature, and we can see how it discovers realities in nature by noticing the parallel between the solution of a difficult perceptual problem and the solution of a scientific one.

Studies of perception have found the remarkable feats of integration that our eyesight performs. Observations of eye motion during the viewing of a scene have shown that our eyes actually perceive a series of snapshots taken from scanning positions at the rate of about three to four shots per second.[9] Yet, our visual image is similar to that of the motion picture where the individual camera shots are seen as one coherent scene. Even more impressive is the way that our perception does not give us the fuzziness of over-lapping snapshots but quickly finds their relationships and forms them into a single sight. To do this, it has had to eliminate a variety of possibilities and bring the many eye movements into a harmony. These efforts of our eyesight are based upon a major assumption akin to the assumption in the making of a scientific discovery, namely, that the things that we see have some reality and coherence. The efforts of our vision to integrate disparate images parallels, in principle, scientists' speculating about strange things in nature to find their hidden significance.

The way in which scientific discovery is an extension of our powers of perception and their tacit features is also shown by the experiments in wearing inverted spectacles. Over seventy years ago Stratton demonstrated that we could wear spectacles that showed everything upside down, yet within a few weeks we could learn to find our way around and eventually perform difficult tasks. Until recently, it was thought that the inverted visual image was switched around to the way we normally see it. When a subject with inverted spectacles was questioned about whether he saw things right way up or upside down, he admitted, after having to think about it, that he saw things upside down still but that the inverted visual image no longer meant that things were upside down.[10] This example shows again the way our human capacity for integrating a variety of puzzling visual clues into an intelligible pattern is related to scientific creativity. Like the wearer of inverted spectacles, faced with a scramble of clues, the scientist establishes a new way of seeing rightly by believing that the clues are not chaotic impressions but real objects yielding order and harmony.

The connection between inverted spectacles and the nature of scientific discovery is clearly put by Polanyi in reference to Einstein's revolutionary move from a Newtonian world of absolute rest to one of relativity of motion and of observer.

It is no accident that the most radical innovation in the history of science appears most similar to the way we acquire the capacity for seeing inverted images rightly. For only a comprehensive problem,

*like relativity, can require that we reorganize such basic concep-
tions as we do in learning to see rightly through inverted spectacles.
Relativity alone involves conceptual innovations as strange and
paradoxical as those we make in righting an inverted vision.*[11]

In both instances, learning to wear inverted spectacles and the
discovery of relativity, a new way of seeing things truly is achieved.
Furthermore, the earlier meaning of terms such as "upside down"
or "space" is changed. All of this also illustrates the way our tacit
powers of knowing assist us in finding a bearing upon reality
through the clues that we receive.

The way discovery takes place through our tacit knowing can be
further clarified by seeing the interplay of imagination and intuition. These two activities are given a more precise role in our
creative acts of intelligence by Polanyi's analysis. Scientific inquiry
begins with the sighting of a good problem. Such a choice is
difficult and a part of scientific genius. There are no rules for this
choice, and Polanyi suggests why in his observation that scientific
inquiry begins with "anticipatory intuition."[12] This anticipating
intuition is a subsidiary awareness of hidden aspects of reality that
prompts our imagination to look in a new direction.

To explain this interplay, Polanyi gives a model of the way
imagination and intuition interact. By intuition he does not mean
the "supreme immediate knowledge" of Leibniz, Spinoza, or Husserl. He means "a skill for guessing with a reasonable chance of
guessing right; a skill guided by an innate sensibility to coherence, improved by schooling."[13] By imagination, he means "all
thoughts of things that are not yet present—or perhaps never to be
present."[14]

One relationship of intuition and imagination is shown in the
wearing of inverted spectacles. At the beginning of the experiment,
the wearer of the spectacles relies upon an awareness of a truer sense
of reality than the images immediately present. He intuits that
there is an order of reality to which he can adjust. His imagination
fixes upon the suggestion of his intuition that there is the
possibility of finding a right way of getting around. Still, the

imagination of the inverted spectacle-wearer cannot give explicit and detailed directions to sight, touch, and hearing, saying, "What we see and hear as above is really below," without hindering smooth performance and progress. But by fixing the attention of his imagination upon the goal of finding the right way around, the inverted spectacle-wearer induces the spontaneous sensory reorientations that lead to his successful adjustment to reality.

Another example of imagination aided by our tacit powers makes this still clearer. To raise an arm requires our imagining the intention of moving it upward.[15] While we can initiate such movement, we cannot explicitly direct the muscle actions and coordination that produce this voluntary exercise. It is also a case of focal awareness of an intention or imagined purpose and of subsidiary awareness of the integrations that enable it to happen.

Using this model, Polanyi suggests that scientific discovery occurs in essentially two steps of the intuition and of the imagination. The first step is the deliberate act of the imagination questing for the hidden reality suggested by the intuition's subsidiary awareness. The second step is in the spontaneous effort of the creative intuition groping toward integration. It is, in principle, in such a way that we, in our ordinary acts of knowing or in our scientific triumphs, gain a knowledge that bears on reality.

There are two features of this process that pertain to deeper problems of our culture as it is affected by the objective ideal. One is that the imagination is guided toward reality by following clues from its own personal intuition. The imaginative effort that focuses on a problem for investigation can do so only because it follows intuitive intimations of the problem's presence and feasibility. This is one dimension of personal knowledge that, while initiated and integrated by ourselves, also discloses the nature of realities independent of us. The second feature of this process is the indeterminate nature of reality itself for which there are no explicit rules to direct us to it. The clues to reality that function in our intuition are not fully explicit but only intimations of an approaching coherence. The processes of integration by which intimations take shape in our imagination at the beginning of a problem or the realization of a discovery are not formalizable. Finally, confidence in the reality of a discovery exceeds the demonstrations that can be explicitly made. Discoveries not only solve problems but also open up potentialities that reorder and redefine our existence in ways yet to be explored. These potentialities of a valid scientific result are also things we know but cannot tell.

The finding and holding of scientific knowledge display a manifold denial of the objective ideal. To many this will still not be convincing because it does not seem to include the role of testing. This role is not ignored, however, but it is placed in the larger context of understanding to which it belongs. Strictly, there are no tests of scientific validity that can directly win assent. Scientific validity or truthfulness is, as we have already seen, an appraisal of the bearing on reality of an idea, and this bearing is dependent upon its tacit foundations. The bearing on reality is an act of personal judgment both for the individual who makes discoveries and for the wider scientific community that evaluates them. Granted that the scientific community has standards of judgment, these standards have to be applied, involving finally our personal powers of perceiving reality.[16] Even the principle of falsifiability is not as certain as many think. While it is true that a single contradiction can logically overthrow a generalization, science does not deal with entities that fit so well into the exactness of logical or mathematical categories. What appears to be a contradiction may only be an apparent contradiction.[17] The question at stake in science is always the nature of reality, and that remains an open question. If we adhered absolutely to the idea of falsifiability, we would be bound to remain within our present definitions and would thereby, foreclose the creative advance that comes with a reordering of our conceptions.

One further demonstration by Polanyi points up the need to rethink the meaning of our scientific procedure. To the extent that science is a body of information and concepts with standard practices for testing and organizing data into intelligible forms, it is also a skill.[18] The use of all of the body of knowledge that is called science depends upon its skillful employment, which is itself an act of tacit knowing. To use a formula or a concept is like using a tool, as we saw in Chapter III. We have to indwell it and allow it to become a part of us in our subsidiary awareness in order to attend focally to the task at hand.[19]

FOUNDATIONS OF TACIT KNOWING

While scientific discovery leads to a revision of our whole paradigm of knowing, it also opens up to our attention the foundations of tacit knowing that make such knowledge possible. The importance of Polanyi's heuristic emphasis is seen in the way that our tacit powers of knowing are rooted in a chain of levels that form our existence.

Investigation shows that all of our principal intellectual capacities are prefigured in lower forms of life. The capacities to read sign-event relations, to engineer means-ends projects, and to be novel by reorganizing and reinterpreting experience are all shared with a wide range of prehuman life.[20] Humans are chiefly advantaged by the feat of their articulate intelligence, which gives them the power of abstract thought and the storing of information for successive generations. Rather than emphasize the difference between animals and humans here, we should notice that our articulate intelligence expressed in words, concepts, and symbols is actually rooted in a prearticulate intelligence. This observation shows that in all of our articulate knowledge there is also involved the tacit coefficient of our prearticulate intelligence.

Also contained in our biological heritage is a groping and finding, a balancing and righting that guides the organism to achievement and self-satisfaction.[21] At this more rudimentary level, the danger of inferential error and systematic error based upon interpretative frameworks is minimal or nonexistent. "Animals can make mistakes; rabbits fall into traps, fish rise to the angler's fly, and such errors are fatal. But animals are exempt from the errors due to elaborate systems of false interpretation, which can be established only in verbal terms."[22] Written within us and exercised on a larger scale is this desire to find our way by satisfying standards and ideas that we set to ourselves.

The satisfaction of self-set standards is interrelated to the environment around organisms and cannot be absolutely self-centered. The organism expresses in its functions what could be called an appraisal of conditions. To ingest something is a rudimentary form of appraisal.[23] What begins as organic need comes to entail a sense of right and wrong in conditions about the organism, such as satisfying nourishment and survival behavior. The satisfaction of needs according to individual standards anticipates human striving to fulfill standards in the finding of and submission to things that are true. Polanyi classifies this growth into three levels: *primordial,* vegetative commitment of a center of being, of function and growth; *primitive,* appraisal by an organism with an active-perceptive center; and *responsible,* appraisal by a consciously deliberating person.[24] This last level accounts for what is described as our universal intent. It is the attempt to satisfy our own standards and needs by the finding of what can be seen and shared by others like ourselves. It is based upon our belief that there exists an independent reality that makes our efforts meaningful and that corresponds to our strivings; and it bears a sense of the hazards of ignoring what is right.

Universal intent presents to us the paradox of self-set standards. Usually, the fulfillment of a standard set by ourselves would be regarded as subjective. But this analysis is erroneous. As we have begun to see above, the logic of living begins involves a quest for the right conditions, ones that satisfy needs and standards, and it is impossible to succeed without a submission to the truth of the independent reality upon which we rely. The final appraisals or commitments of organisms are not subjective but actions directed toward what is true. We and other living beings survive by this alliance that we make with reality through our self-directed exploring.

The paradox of self-set standards places before us one of the central difficulties of our scientific outlook. If the scientific out-look means only knowledge that is impersonal, detached, deter-mined solely by the object and not by the subject at all, is true, then we can have no genuine knowledge. The investigation of the knowing activity itself shows that we are called upon by our nature to search for the truth and to state our findings. This seeking with universal intent is an obligation that we place upon ourselves. Our seeking and our satisfaction with what is true lead us to make this search for the truth into a standard that we continue to follow. From our quests and applications of what we find for ourselves grows "a firmament of standards" that becomes our tradition and culture.[25] The study of knowledge confronts us with the fact that only by relying upon ourselves and the achievements of culture that arise from our knowing are we equipped to pursue the truth. We are presented with a background of opportunities and dangers as a platform on which to carry on our search. Whatever knowledge we accept as true carries always our judgment that it fulfills our universal intent. Whoever judges himself or another also has to judge by his or her own universal intent.

These examples of the nature of knowing explain why Polanyi was led to the theory of tacit knowing, a theory that accounts for our personal participation in the finding and holding of knowl-edge. When we adequately understand this theory, we can see more clearly how a proper understanding of knowledge guides us to live within the bounds that we conceive to be true, but which might conceivably be false. This is a situation that calls for our acceptance of responsibility with no guarantee that we or our civilization will be right. It is a situation of hope acting on the confidence of our and others' universal intent.

It is often said that we cannot tell anyone how to make discoveries; they cannot be predicted or guaranteed. This statement becomes trivial in the face of Polanyi's thought that does tell us in a fundamental way about the nature of discovery. While it does not guide us to the solution of a specific problem X by doing ABC, it does show us the principles of discovery within which specific discoveries occur. The difficulty of the objective ideal is that it unwittingly denies the way in which our heuristic passions have to be conducted within a framework that cannot be made fully explicit, and a framework that is imposed upon us by ourselves.

THE PANORAMA OF TACIT KNOWING

Polanyi's heuristic philosophy begins as an alteration of our common epistemological paradigm, but it leads to a new vision of our place in the universe and the nature of the universe itself. Once Polanyi had uncovered the logic of scientific knowing with the centrality of discovery, he also found that the way we know turns out to reflect the structure of our being.[26] As such, the theory of tacit knowing becomes a guide to the fundamental rethinking of our existence.

1. *The Hierarchies of Life and Human Responsibility*
This new vision begins with the seeing of human life as the highest level yet achieved in an evolutionary hierarchy that follows principles similar to those of tacit knowing. As the highest level of this stratified universe, humans are faced with the challenge of accepting responsibly their role in such a scheme. These notions, too, like Polanyi's attack upon the objective ideal, conflict with some of the most widely accepted views of human nature and destiny.

Polanyi's case reveals the false objectivity in our scientific sense of what is important. First, it is seen that we do not take a strictly objective view of the universe in our knowledge. If things were studied strictly on an objective scale, our human existence and concerns would scarcely be considered since our place in the span of time and size of the universe is infinitesimal. Most of our time on an exact objective scale would be devoted to the study of interstellar dust.[27] Obviously, this standard is not applied. The theory of evolution is a good example of its denial. If we studied on a strictly objective scale those forms of life that have survival value due to natural selection, human life would scarcely command attention.

Human life today appears to have less probability of survival than insects, yet this does not prevent our immense interest in human origins, existence, and problems. Against such an objective study of natural life, we would have to say that it would be "the height of intellectual perversion to renounce, in the name of scientific objectivity, our position as the highest form of life on earth, and our own advent by a process of evolution as the most important problem of evolution."[28]

Second, it is a glaring omission for scientific views, particularly evolutionary theory, to fail to give an account, in their descriptions of the world, of persons who could find and hold such ideas. Yet this fact prevails so long as scientists and their unwitting followers contend that humans do not have minds or that what appears as a mind is a fictional name for physical and chemical reactions in a highly complex machine. We are in a world of knowledge without genuine knowers, a situation of absurdity. It is such views that have contributed to our homelessness and which are refuted by Polanyi's philosophy.

The chief principle of tacit knowing, as we have seen it, is the way a coherent knowledge of something is achieved by our relying on one level, the subsidiary awareness, for attending to another level, the focal target. This principle suggests a dynamic and purposeful way in which various levels of reality, parts and wholes, can relate in establishing diverse achievements or comprehensive entities.

An elementary example of this principle is the making and use of bricks.[29] At the lowest level is the raw material and then comes the brickmaker. Above the brickmaker is the architect who relies on the brickmaker, and above the architect is the town planner who sets limits to the architect's work. For each of these four successive levels there are four corresponding levels of operational principles and rules. The laws of physics and chemistry govern the raw material of the bricks; technology governs the art of brickmaking; architecture guides the builders; and the standards of town planning govern the town planners. What we see already is the way that lower conditions are sufficient for their own level but depend on principles above them for the achievement of the comprehensive feat of building. A reduction of building to only the principles of physics and chemistry would prevent the construction itself.

Polanyi gives a number of examples of this problem, but one that is most telling concerns our achievement of meaningful speech.[30] In this case we have five levels, not including the levels leading up to the person speaking: 1) voice, 2) words, 3) sentences, 4) style, and 5) literary composition. Each of these levels is governed by its own laws as prescribed by the principles of: 1) phonetics, 2) lexicography, 3) grammar, 4) stylistics, and 5) literary criticism. These levels and their principles form a hierarchy leading to meaningful speech by having each level under the control of the next higher level.

The obvious yet important point here is that we live in a world of hierarchies that are governed by the principle of dual control. Each level is subject first to the laws or principles that apply directly to it, but it is also subject to the laws or principles of the achievement or comprehensive entity formed by it. This observation leads then to the conclusion that "the operations of a higher level cannot be accounted for by the laws governing its particulars forming a lower level."[31]

When this understanding is applied to modern biology, its significance becomes more clear. Modern biology, particularly through the influence of molecular biology, has aimed to explain all of the phenomena of life in terms of physics and chemistry. Such an endeavor means that ultimately life is to be reduced to the atomic level of the Laplacean model. Polanyi's notion counters this effort by saying that what biologists are in fact doing is attempting an explanation of living "machinery based on the laws of physics and chemistry."[32] The error of biologists is in thinking that an organism based upon laws of physics and chemistry can be entirely explicable in terms of physics and chemistry, which is like thinking that a building of bricks can be explained entirely in terms of the elements of bricks.

To make his distinction between levels more intelligible, Polanyi speaks of "the principle of marginal control."[33] Marginal control is the influence exerted by a higher level of principles upon the particulars forming it. A machine offers a simple illustration of this principle. Here we find that a typewriter can be described in terms of its physical and chemical properties, but we do not have a typewriter unless we also have the operational principles of the typing machine.[34] These principles harness the laws of physics and chemistry in the service of the engineering principles that constitute a typewriter. In effect, the principle of marginal control organizes the boundary conditions of the lower level that have been left indeterminate by nature.

The direction of Polanyi's argument is already clear though not presented here in detail. In order to understand ourselves, our world, and how we can know both, we must acknowledge the way hierarchies are formed. The universe, from inanimate matter up to human life, presents a highly complex and varied picture, yet it is one of ascending levels of order in which new operational principles come into play as the lower conditions are presented that make them possible.

Polanyi especially considers the work of molecular biology in its conception of the genetic code as illustrating in a living system the presence of a hierarchy of operational principles.[35] DNA is an information system and as such has to operate under a system of dual control. As we saw above in our analysis of levels of speech, a code that conveys information is not reducible to its physical and chemical level without giving up its nature as information. Such a reduction would be like reducing meaningful words on a printed page to the physical and chemical elements that compose the words on the page.[36] For DNA to function as a blueprint that will initiate and control the growth of an organism, two conditions besides the physical and chemical components must be present. One is the possibility of these physical and chemical components' being arranged in a meaningful rather than a random way. The second is that operational principles exist that can harness these elements into the possible meaningful pattern. Such requirements may seem to many to be simply a part of physics and chemistry anyway.[37] To Polanyi, it is not a slight matter since it touches one of the central issues: whether human persons or life itself can be reduced to a

[97]

collocation of atomic particles without a loss of important levels of reality.

Polanyi traces a new theme in the theory of evolution by his particular way of viewing the ascending levels through principles of dual control.[38] This theme focuses upon centers of individuality in contrast with the usual concern of natural selection with populations. Sentience or self-directing action begins far down the scale of life. Each level of development provides conditions that allow for marginal principles to come into action, giving a boundary to the lower conditions and directing them to particular functions. These levels of growth lead in a process of intensification to the appearance of sentient human life. What is novel here is that Polanyi has aligned his theory of knowing with the emergence of human life so that it gives an account of the rise of intelligent human life. Current theory of evolution with its emphasis upon "changes due to the selective advantage of random mutations cannot acknowledge this problem."[39] Hence, it is not surprising that modern biology has been unable to account for the rise of intelligent human life except as the blind working of "chance and necessity."[40]

Human life stands at the top of a long story of achievements, of biotic changes that involved increasing subordination of lower levels to the service of higher ones. With the rise of sentience, the possibility of error began. With the rise of human beings, the possibility of inferential error began. Each higher level of life bears an increase in the potentiality for failure as its interpretative capacities enlarge.[41] Human life is then faced with two conditions which the objective ideal has attemped to deny with destructive consequences. The first is that we are by nature creatures who live and know only by indwelling. Our living individuality is not an explicit map of atomic particles, but a hierarchy of levels. Just as we cannot simultaneously attend to the meaning of a sentence and analyze its syntax, neither can we affirm our own selfhood and detail its physics and chemistry. We are comprehensive entities that cannot be specified completely by our parts. To acknowledge ourselves or other persons, we have to acknowledge an integral awareness. Second, all of our knowledge is related to the same principle that our being is, namely, it is the indwelling of clues through our subsidiary awareness in order that we may attend to our focal target. This structure of knowing and being points to a directionality in our very nature. It is a groping of matter, at first, toward higher levels that enables thought, and it is next a groping of thought toward reality.

We are faced then with learning anew the logic and limitations of our knowing and being. It is a logic that tells us that we cannot make progress by trying to escape from the bodily roots of all of our knowing or from the peculiar place of our thought in the development of living beings. Knowledge is truly personal knowledge in that it is an act of ourselves and also of our reliance upon myriad centers of thought that have gone before us. This potentiality of a lower level being harnessed to serve a higher one has led after millions of years to a human person who can also harness his or her bodily capacities to the service of ideas, ideas that in turn serve at each stage as one level opening up the possibility of a higher one, and of a deeper knowledge of reality.

To assimilate the implications of a heuristic philosophy, Polanyi suggests that we need a new conception of our human nature as "a Society of Explorers."[42] The consequences of the scientific outlook and its objective ideal were twofold. They led to a mistaken notion of knowledge, and they led to a destructive attempt at progress. Once knowledge became impersonal and detached, it led to the questioning of all traditional authority and its eventual replacement with moral inversion, the passionate pursuit of disguised moral goals without a guiding moral framework. The developing of a theory of knowledge from the actual process of scientific discovery has disclosed the impossibility of truly succeeding in these objectivist attempts. "We start the pursuit of discovery by pouring ourselves into the subsidiary elements of a problem and we continue to spill ourselves into further clues as we advance further, so that we arrive at discovery fully committed to it as an aspect of reality."[43] These discoveries that we hold to be true, so far as we can presently see, create in us a new existence. In this sense,

[99]

our own heuristic efforts come before the truth that we establish and make our own.

Far from showing that we are the beginning or author of our own values, the way of scientific discovery and other discoveries shows that we advance by relying upon the current state of knowledge as the source of intuitions that guide our imagination. It also shows that science, from one perspective, is filled with inarticulate premises, the presence of which are the openings for future discoveries.[44] Or stated more positively, every instance of scientific reality presents an indeterminate range of future manifestations beckoning for further exploration and including the potential of revising even our own standpoint, such as happened in the movement from Newtonian to Einsteinian conceptions. It is the greatest folly to project a method of discovery in knowledge that claims to begin from absolute zero. For this reason, Polanyi is in disagreement with the existential belief that "man makes himself."[45]

The organization and government of the scientific community that Polanyi recognized in the struggle for the freedom of science give a picture of the way humans, immersed in thought, gain and share a knowledge of reality that they respect and follow. It is a community of general rather than "dogmatic" authority.[46] Belief in the bearing of its ideas and methods upon reality sustains and guides the community. Its pursuit is upheld by a common loyalty to the truth illuminated by its way of study; students, teachers, and researchers check and criticize each other from this point of reference. To submit to science and to do its service is to submit not to the heroes or their theories but to the truth of reality that it is believed that they reveal.[47] Because of this transcendent loyalty to the truth, science contains its own basis for renewal and growth.

Transferring this theory to society in general, we are called by the nature of knowing to accept the responsibility to seek the truth and to state our findings. There are many ways of knowing reality and many levels to our understanding of it. These differences make for a variety of studies and investigations. Still, these various approaches are bound together by a single structure of knowing, tacit

[100]

knowing. Their joint task is to carry forth their individual pursuits, with influence upon each other like overlapping neighborhoods and mutual control.[48]

2. The Paths of Explorers

One of the most striking features of Polanyi's understanding of tacit knowing is the way it illuminates the distinctive heuristic roles of various fields of study. The nature of the reality discovered in science is one that allows for a greater degree of control and of description in comparison to the reality discovered by art where we are more left to our interior sense of understanding. In his last book, *Meaning*, consisting of lectures given at the University of Texas and at the University of Chicago, Polanyi makes this difference into a part of his comprehensive theory. This serves to demonstrate how a Society of Explorers is a joint enterprise with each field bearing a significant responsibility for the growth of thought and understanding.

To clarify the difference between the sciences and the other fields, Polanyi notices that scientific knowledge does not "carry us away" in the same degree as art, morality, and religion do.[49] This difference is further illuminated by Polanyi's distinguishing two poles in knowing, one called "self-centered" and the other, "self-giving."[50] The "self-centered" is that form of knowing that is more confined to perception in its observational aspect and to the gaining of the kind of knowledge that we call "scientific." This form of knowledge does not depend as much upon our knowledge of it for its existence. One way in which this is manifested daily is in our employment of all sorts of scientific knowledge in our use of technology. This knowledge is effective without our paying specific attention to it. Few people think of their constant use of mechanical principles discovered by science when they turn on an electric switch or drive a car. On the other hand, a painting, a poem, or a symphony requires our attention in a different way in order for it to have a significant existence. We have to notice it, follow it, and try to fathom its depth.

[101]

This difference helps us to see why Polanyi speaks of works of art, morality, and religion as "carrying us away." These are forms of knowing that increase our involvement in significant ways.

Through a series of diagrams and of examples Polanyi elaborates the range of meaning that comes to us through various types of knowing.[51] Beginning with scientific or "self-centered" knowing, Polanyi shows that what we know of it focally is of more interest to us than the subsidiary clues that form it. The subsidiary clues hold interest for us mostly in the object upon which they bear. Thus stars, crystals, physiognomies, and cells are of more intrinsic interest to us than the numerous clues we indwell in order to see them. "Self-centered" here does not contain any value judgment or connotation. but it refers to the way that the subsidiary awareness functions mainly in the focal awareness. Polanyi diagrams this self-centered integration in this way:

$$\text{integration} = \begin{matrix} \text{-ii} & \quad \text{+ii} \\ \xrightarrow{\hspace{2cm}} & \\ \text{s} & \quad \text{f} \end{matrix}$$

ii stands for intrinsic interest,- for a lack of this interest, + for the presence of this interest, s for subsidiary, and f for focal.[52]

But as expected, a self-giving interest below will show a "+" in the subsidiary clues. This happens, Polanyi explains, because the subsidiary gathers up elements of significance to us over a lifetime. These are elements with memories and associations that are important to us in themselves. He makes this distinction of the self-giving knowing vivid by considering how a symbol may lack interest in itself, but because it has subsidiary clues that are of interest to us carries us away. Such an example is a flag or the tomb of a loved one. Here the diagram is drawn as follows:

$$\text{integration} = \begin{matrix} \text{+ii} & \quad \text{-ii} \\ \xrightarrow{\hspace{2cm}} & \\ \text{s} & \quad \text{f}^{53} \end{matrix}$$

[102]

Still, the power of a symbol is not yet fully represented in this case, for a symbol is much richer than the second diagram above indicates. An effective symbol is one that we surrender ourselves to as expressing a meaning about and for us. Polanyi therefore revises the diagram to show that it is not only an integration of subsidiaries that is of interest to us but also one that involves our own existence to some extent. The diagram then becomes as follows:

$$\text{integration of} = +ii \quad \overset{\frown}{\bigcirc} \quad \text{-ii}$$

$$\text{our existence} \quad s \qquad\qquad f$$

The "somersault" represents the way our own self is gathered up into the subsidiaries.[54]

The process displayed by Polanyi in these diagrams throws light on a frequently debated phenomenon, the reality of symbols. From his analysis it is quite clear that the symbol is in one sense artificial and transient, of no intrinsic interest in itself. Nevertheless, the symbol bears on reality because it integrates impressions, memories, affections, and so on, that belong to us. In this way, the diffuse experiences of a lifetime may be brought to a focus that allows us to give ourselves to a meaning that we could not have otherwise known. Now an ancient question about the reality of symbols is answered, for we can see through Polanyi's analysis that to think of the flag or of the tomb in terms of the material parts that compose it is to focus upon a lower level of reality rather than upon the new one to which these material parts contribute. The reality, to which the flag points or for which it functions as a subsidiary, is of a higher level.

The way our knowledge of reality grows, as one level provides conditions for another, is now more apparent. We have just recognized a fundamental way in which we begin to move from self-centered integrations, those mainly of the scientific kind, to self-giving integrations, those that arise through symbols. There is still a deeper or richer explanation to be had by turning to rituals and metaphors, and with these distinctions in mind we are prepared to see the full range of possible levels of meaning, from science through the arts to religion.

The nature of a ritual is midway between a symbol and a metaphor.[55] A ritual carries us away in a manner similar to that of a symbol, except that its power is heightened by the resemblance in its actions to the history from which it comes and the meaning toward which it points. This resemblance can be seen in baptism, which both remembers an event and points to a reality of purification.

A metaphor has a more striking means of comparison than a ritual. Instead of taking things that are seen to have a more obvious resemblance, it takes things that are not so obvious and brings them together in a powerful comparison. Polanyi views this distinctive characteristic of metaphor as an integration of incompatibles.[56] One of the examples that Polanyi uses to illustrate this characteristic feature is from Ezra Pound's poem "In a Station of the Metro:"

The apparition of these faces in the crowd,
Petals on a wet, black bough.[57]

The combination of images is a novel integration of separate elements into a coherent picture. Another illustration used by Polanyi shows the spectacular way that metaphor can function.

Not all the waters of the rough rude sea
Can wash the balm from an anointed king.[58]

This passionate expression by Richard II in Shakespeare's play shows the semantic mechanism of integration of incompatibles, and the resulting new meaning is by the same mechanism as that by which a flag is made to symbolize a country, except that we become more involved or carried away by a metaphor than we do by a symbol. Polanyi diagrams this example of meaning as follows:

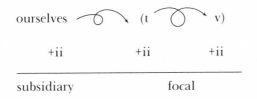

$$+ii \qquad\qquad +ii \qquad\qquad +ii$$

subsidiary   focal

t stands for the tenor of the metaphor, and v stands for the vehicle of the metaphor.[59]

The diagram indicates the increased capacity of metaphor to carry us away by the power of two additional features. Besides our intrinsic interest in all of its aspects about our own existence, there is the mood and meaning that it bears. The king expresses the feeling of frustration and defiance known to us all in the tenor of the metaphor, "Not all the waters of the rough rude sea. . . ." and expresses the failure of any earthly power to change what has been done in the vehicle of the metaphor, "Can wash the balm from an anointed king."

Art is similar to metaphor in its ability to carry us away and as an integration of incompatibles, but Polanyi notices in it an additional feature that adds to its peculiar power.[60] Art takes up elements from the world of nature, yet it detaches and distorts them into integrations that catch up emotion and imagination. These integrations are transnatural meanings, meanings built upon things in nature but rising above them. Two examples make this transnatural form of integration of meanings clear. First is the way in which even a representative painting has a frame or background that clearly indicates that it is a painting. Sometimes this feature is the flatness of the canvas, or some other denotation that sets off the painting from nature, and of which we are only subsidiarily aware as we attend to the comprehensive character of the painting.[61] A second example is the art of stagecraft.[62] Plays, too, are based upon things in nature and human affairs. Still, when viewing the dramatization of a murder onstage, we are not moved to intervene, call the police, or take action because we are aware of the frame of the work of art. Again, we enter into a transnatural integration of

[105]

meaning that allows us to behold a meaning bearing upon ourselves and nature and yet is above both.

Polanyi gives the following diagram of this instance of integration of meaning:

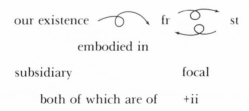

our existence   fr   st

embodied in

subsidiary   focal

both of which are of   +ii

fr stands for frame, st for story, and by "both of which are of intrinsic interest," Polanyi means our subsidiary and our focal awareness.[63]

This diagram shows how the canvas or the stage is embodied in the "story" which we focally perceive, but the additional somersaulting arrow shows that the "story" is also carrying an awareness of the frame. We have then both the meaning of the story with its power and also a realism that does not lead us to mistake the painting or the representation of murder for its natural type.

The complex developments of the achievement of meaning through tacit knowing lead toward Polanyi's understanding of morality and religion. He has not given a diagram at this point, but Harry Prosch has constructed one showing the implications of Polanyi's thought. Consideration of this last picture will complete the survey of self-centered and self-giving acts of knowing. Prosch's diagram is as follows:

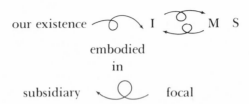

our existence   I   M   S

embodied
in

subsidiary   focal

I stands for institutions in the place of frame, and M S for moral standards in place of story in the previous example.[64]

The significance of this further development of Polanyi's conceptions is to make clearer the way our highest obligations and understandings are rooted in our tacit knowing, bear upon reality, and serve as our guide for further growth and exploration. Institutions and traditions are transnatural creations or integrations that gather up and bind us together into a society. The institution or tradition is not able to serve fully unless it also embodies and is embodied by rights and duties. A frame functions this way for a painting and a stage for drama. Here the diagram means that we cannot have moral standards and aspirations without the institutions that are their frame nor can we have institutions and civil life unless these standards are also embodied in the society.[65] A stage does not carry us away unless the play makes use of the artificial advantage of the stage. Likewise, institutions and traditions cannot serve us unless we choose to be guided by the ideals to which they point.

Thus, we arrive at a point where it is epistemologically shown that "self-giving" integrations are the means by which humans have risen far beyond the prearticulate intelligence of their animal ancestors. These integrations also go beyond the "self-centered" ones that describe science because of the increased intrinsic interest that comes from their bearing upon ourselves and reality. Our most universal and compelling knowledge and standards share the same personal foundation as scientific knowledge; the difference in some other areas such as art and religion is that we face the demand upon ourselves that these creative integrations make. These are not less true, but more challenging.

This final development also shows in a stronger way the impossibility of holding to any knowledge, from "self-centered" to "self-giving," without its tacit and personal foundation. The modern scientific outlook, with its objective ideal that passionately seeks to found right and truth upon a principle independent of our fundamental action and participation, is not only false but is destructive of the nature of the creative process that has enabled human life to integrate incompatibles into visions that can guide us.

Such a panorama of knowledge built upon the principle of tacit knowing becomes a permanent challenge to the human communi- ty to acknowledge that we alone have the responsibility for seeking the truth and upholding it with a universal intent that will expect its revision and renewal in future discoveries. Knowing is an unformalizable process striving toward an achievement that also is not fully specifiable; accordingly, it is also attributed to the agency of a center seeking satisfaction in the light of its own standards.

Looking back, this process began with the eons of emergence. The searching movements by which worms explore the way in front of them are precursors of the far more effective exploratory movements and functions of visual, auditory, and olfactory percep- tion. The use of sense organs extended the animal's area of intelli- gent control into surrounding space. "But seeing is foreseeing and is hence also believing; perception involves judgment and the possi- bility of error. Therefore, as the personhood of our ancestors was enriched and expanded by the power of new senses, it was intensi- fied still further in undertaking to control new hazards."[66] The polarity of an intelligent center in a vast range of reality led to the structure of tacit knowing. Relying upon our bodies as the instru- ments by which we explore the world, we were formed so that our knowledge will always be a risk and a hope. To try to escape from this opportunity through an objective ideal is to deny our own nature and the long story of evolution. Instead, we are called to accept our responsibility in a "heuristic field."[67]

The assumption of a heuristic field summarizes how we gain knowledge and hold it. We do this by our attraction to what is real, yet we can never fully specify. To say that something is a fact or is true is to say that others ought to believe it.[68] Just as knowledge can never be made fully explicit, so never can the ideals of our society be fully realized. To the extent that our moral and religious standards bear upon reality, there will always be an unspecifiable and an unrealizable dimension. A society of free and creative persons will be one that has learned to live within these limitations. It will respect and seek the truth, and it will hold to it because of the indeterminate range of manifestations that the truth may yield in

[108]

the future. Such a society is a free community whose sovereign is the pursuit of truth. It is a Society of Explorers freed from the absurdity of the objective ideal and able to rely upon the frailties and strengths of its tradition and its heroes in an unlimited expedition into the ranges of reality.

v. Invitation to Explorers

EXPLORATIONS IN THE MAKING

Michael Polanyi's heuristic philosophy alters not only the dominant models of knowing and of human creativity but also our understanding of the vocation of our culture. From the centrality of the human agent who inquires and creates grows his vision of a Society of Explorers. It is a society of humans placed in the midst of potential discoveries, which offer them numberless problems.[1] It is a society where each human is given a calling to be an active center pursuing the truth with universal intent. The human is called with his or her whole range of being to strive for integration, intelligence, and understanding. Acceptance of this calling is a choice that only each individual can make, but at the same time, it is a surrender to a belief in the presence of a hidden reality that others can share. Such a surrender, while personal, is an opening of our being to the current teachings and standards in the social lore, to factual conditions, and to practical and intellectual disciplines in which we live and which lead on to unknown truths that may alter or dissent from the very teachings that engendered them.

This calling to discovery is one that asks us both to rely upon all our powers, passional and rational, and to acknowledge at the same time the limits of all our powers. The risk of error and of failure is always with us, but it is not total. As the structure of tacit knowing makes clear, we are aided in our efforts by a contact with reality that awakens and beckons us onward. The acceptance of this calling places upon us the burden and the opportunity of responsibility for seeking truth and stating our findings. If we are to be intelligently human, we cannot do otherwise.

The heuristic emphasis of Polanyi's philosophy is prophetic. It pioneers and expresses a new direction of consciousness already in the making. Reorientation is beginning and may be seen in the heuristic impulses now at work across a whole field of disciplines.[2] The emergence of a new paradigm and the growth of the premises of a Society of Explorers are seen in the rising number of critiques of scientism, in the reexamination of the conceptions of life from the biological to the human sciences, and in the comprehensive philosophical reorientation underway from philosophy to the arts. The survey that follows indicates the foresight of Polanyi's heuristic philosophy and the contribution his philosophy is making to this wider movement.

TRADITIONAL PHILOSOPHY

The motivation of Polanyi's philosophical efforts is to provide a general service for society by curbing the scientific outlook and voicing our decisive beliefs. When this vocation was expressed in his Gifford Lectures of 1951–52, comprehensive philosophy was in disrepute. Analytical linguistic philosophy called for the limitation of philosophy to the uses of language, and existentialism distrusted general views as abstractions lacking the reality of individual and authentic experience. Because Polanyi recognized the central problem in the philosophical crisis, his thought is a contribution to all areas: traditional philosophy, analytical philosophy, and existentialism.

Helmut Kuhn shows how Polanyi revived the metaphysical mode of thought by carrying out an encounter with problems, facts, and experiences rather than by limiting himself to the conventional approaches of the academic philosophical tradition.[3] By starting from an original point, namely, the process of discovery in natural science, Polanyi is able to achieve philosophic universality and relevance. Kuhn sets forth his appraisal first by showing the ontological import of Polanyi's epistemology and by showing second its bearing on the problem of historicism consequent to Hegel's influence.

Kuhn shows the ontological significance of Polanyi's thought by relating it to the classical tradition. Instead of regarding physics as all of nature, Polanyi returns physics to its status as a human enterprise viewing a stratum of nature.[4] The lust-for-power view of scientific achievement is also rejected by Polanyi and replaced by a view of science as personal dedication to genuine "objective knowledge."[5] But this objective knowledge is not a detached object, it is an intelligent personal contact with reality. Knowledge for Polanyi has ontological significance in two ways: 1) as fecundity, the opening to wider contact with reality, which makes the researcher and the discoverer more like a "gold digger than an architect";[6] and 2) as analogy to being, the necessity of indwelling in order to know, which shows that the mind-body relationship is a parallel to the stratification of reality.[7] "Knowledge and reality are tied together by a natural affinity of structure. . . ."[8] When we discover the structure of knowing, we are thrust into the all-comprehensive community of things and also assigned a place within the realm of living beings. For Polanyi, evolution, instead of submerging humans in nature, shows the transformation from animal purposive effort to passionate commitment to an "absolute demand."[9]

Kuhn is very perceptive in stressing that Polanyi is not concerned with proving the existence of an independent reality nor with upholding solipsism. For him, knowledge always means coming to grips with reality in a framework of personal commitment. When we assert the truth of something, we assert that it bears on reality. But the meaning of truth is only intelligible to one who acknowldges the absolute demand made on him by the truth. Only for personal knowledge does knowledge reveal its ontological import.[10]

Polanyi, says Kuhn, regains the path of classical metaphysics without being fully aware of it.[11] Because he did not follow current philosophical method, he caught knowledge in action rather than an abstract idea of it. Like Plato and Aristotle, he followed Socrates' example of choosing a skill as the point of departure. For Plato and Aristotle, the skill was art, for Polanyi, science.[12]

Polanyi's contribution to the problem of historicism is also a substantial one. The attempt of the history of philosophy to find meaning by discovery of the immutable principles at work in the process of history was driven into retreat by the recognition of the relativism of the observer of history. Historicism became an attempt to study all phenomena as historically determined but without imposing the values of the historian. The predicament of this development is aptly described by Kuhn.[13] When historicism admitted relativism into its position, it actually meant that a knowledge that was relevant was also personal but probably untrue or distorted. Such knowledge becomes undesirable and unconvincing. The only alternative is likewise unattractive, namely, a knowledge that is irrelevant but impersonal and free of historical bias since it cannot take up the matrix of our present lives. Truth at this price becomes abstract and extraneous. The importance of Polanyi is that personal knowledge steers a way between the two extremes of the problem. It rejects not only as useless but also as impossible the ideal of objective history. At the same time, through its grasp of tradition and the ontological character of knowledge, personal knowledge avoids the subjectivism and relativism of knowledge that is regarded as untrue. The problem of historicism is another form of the subject-object dichotomy that has become the plight of modern thought. Polanyi saw the basic problem in this whole field and broke with it. For this reason, his work is both a recognition of the nature of the philosophical crisis and a successful breaking of the stalemate.

ANALYTICAL PHILOSOPHY

The prophetic power of Polanyi's philosophy is also seen in the movement of analytical linguistic philosophy from its early background and attempt at "unbridled lucidity" to its growing recognition of the indeterminacies of language and meaning. From the start, Polanyi knew that a criterion of exactness and of absolute precision in science would deny us the most valuable discoveries and conceptions. Science proceeds with an appearance of precision that is only intelligible when seen against the background of assumptions, presuppositions, and intuitions upon which a scientist tacitly relies and can only vaguely define. A scientist's work is a highly developed and disciplined skill. In this sense, Polanyi expressed about science a characteristic of language noticed by the later Wittgenstein, namely, that it is like tools in a box and there is more of an art than a rule to applying them.[14]

Viewed from this broadening of the investigation of language by later analytical philosophy, Polanyi's critique and philosophical direction is supported, and scholars now find major affinities between his thought and such figures as Wittgenstein, Austin, and Wisdom. Cahal Daly has particularly developed these connections showing that analytical philosophy, in some of its major voices, moved toward Polanyi's conceptions without knowing it.[15] Daly finds, for example, an elaborate parallel in the thrust of Wittgenstein's later thought and the concept held by Polanyi. Wittgenstein wanted to avoid the monistic and monopolistic tendencies of language and thought and to recover the diversity and variety of reality.[16] Polanyi's attack upon the oversimplifications of positivism is similar to Wittgenstein's criticism of positivism as "a bewitchment of our intelligence."[17] What Polanyi actually accom-. plished in his work was to show that the way scientists use terms is different from the way the positivist philosophers of science use them, a feat close to the concerns of Wittgenstein.[18] Instead of the exactness and the objectivity portrayed by the positivist, Polanyi showed what Wittgenstein came to see as one of the central and deep problems of all knowledge, namely, the inherent ambiguity of language.[19]

The parallels between Wittgenstein and Polanyi are found in three areas. First is their similarity in technique. Wittgenstein asked "to look at the facts," and this is the tack that Polanyi uses in his refutation of the positivist idea of simplicity.[20] Polanyi also appeals from "meaning" to "use" in his study of the operational principles of language.[21] Finally, the similarity in their technique is seen in the way Polanyi enlarges the rational meaning of science by doing what Wittgenstein meant when he spoke of giving scientific expressions meaning in the "stream of life."[22]

The second parallel is in their understanding of the nature of language. The most striking similarity between Wittgenstein and Polanyi is that they "both see language as meaningful only within the wider context of culture, tradition, and ways of human living."[23] This agreement is found also in their recognition of the role of Gestalt in our knowing. Wittgenstein used the Gestalt expression of "perceptual shift" to describe the noticing of a new aspect, which is similar to Polanyi's notion that a new way of perceiving a group of clues may enable us to grasp new areas of reality.[24] This insight into the nature of language, as Daly points out, is convincingly shown by T. S. Kuhn in the idea of a paradigm shift in which the meaning of "space," for example, changes from the Newtonian view to the Einsteinian.[25]

The third parallel is found in the approach of Wittgenstein and Polanyi to the understanding of mind, behaviorism, and solipsism. Both deny the mind-body dichotomy in knowledge. Wittgenstein rejected philosophy as introspection and showed that mental processes are not two things, a public thing and a private thing. He saw that the mental is in the physical; that it is embodied rationality, which is like Polanyi's thesis on the structure of tacit knowing.[26] Both are similar in their answer to a behavioristic model of the mind that equates the mind with its workings. Rather, the mind is the comprehensive manifestation of these workings. ". . . It is always the mind itself that we know primarily; any knowledge of its workings is derivative, vague, and uncertain."[27] Finally, Wittgenstein and Polanyi are parallel in their refutation of solipsism. "For Polanyi, as for Wittgenstein, 'private language' about 'private sensations' is meaningless."[28] Knowledge and language for Polanyi are characterized by social encounter and interaction, as seen in his display of the essential roles of conviviality, community, and consensus in knowledge.

Other connections between Polanyi and analytical philosophy follow a direction similar to Wittgenstein's. The late Ian Ramsey showed how John Austin and Polanyi share a critical attitude toward the ideal of scientific detachment.[29] Both reject the view of the world as one of bare atomic facts or sense data and see that all assertions have a self-involving character. William Poteat shows in a creative synthesis the close relation between analytical philosophy's concern with language and phenomenology's understanding of the modes of our being, the way Polanyi's thought is an example of our mode of being in the world.[30] Poteat points out the danger of trying to analyze too much with words and neglecting other clues such as odors and feelings.[31] Poteat notes that central to all language games is the person. The most important fact about logical neighborhoods and conceptual topographies is that they are inhabited by "sayers."[32] The force of Poteat's Polanyian synthesis is to show that there is a common epistemological ground between eschatological myths, stories, history, and ordinary articulate forms in that they share the same form of personal backing to attain their meaning.[33] The importance of the person and of tacit knowing was also intuited by John Wisdom in his comments on Wittgenstein's method. Wisdom spoke of the limitations of articulate thought and the necessity for personal involvement by "giving

[117]

our minds to incidents and incidents, whether they be as familiar as the fall of an apple or as recondite as the Michelson-Morley experiment, or the disorder of a man like poor Dr. Schreber."[34]

EXISTENTIALISM

Of Polanyi's relation to existentialism, Marjorie Grene has given the most decisive account. In a creative and careful analysis of Sartre's *Being and Nothingness*, she has shown how Sartre's work is a protest against Cartesian dualism but fatefully on Cartesian ground leaving us in the tragic "to-and-fro" of our era.[35] Instead of solving our problem, Sartre exemplifies the modern impasse. Sartre's dichotomy of the "in-itself" and the "for-itself" shows that we are a negation, a disintegration if we begin from the Cartesian separation of knowing and being. Then Grene brilliantly shows that the solution to Sartre's predicament is to replace the hectic "to-and-fro" with Polanyi's "from-to" relation of tacit knowing.[36]

Another study of Polanyi and existentialism indicates the positive relationship that develops when existentialism moves beyond a world of absurdity to the risk of meaning. Donald Millholand in a study of Albert Camus and Michael Polanyi focuses on their relationship through the problem of modern nihilism.[37] According to Millholand, the absurd of Sartre is a corollary of the positivism that denies any essential meaning that is not empirically verifiable. Aesthetic, ethical, metaphysical, or religious values are seen as senseless. From this assumption that there are no essential values, Sartre goes on to claim that the human person is free to create his or her own values. But Camus finds Sartre's existential response nihilistic, a destructive attempt to achieve absolute power and freedom. Hence Camus seeks to go beyond nihilism, and he does it in a way akin to Polanyi's thought.

Camus, in the face of absurdity, affirms an essential meaning to life. While the empirical and natural world does not establish values for us, it teaches us our limits. Moreover, we find in the acceptance of our limits a grace that enables us to live. Camus shows that people will revolt in the name of moderation or of life when faced with brutality and absurdity. This risk of affirmation of meaning is the move beyond nihilism that Millholand sees as similar to Polanyi's. Polanyi accepts limitations of our knowing, but he rejects the skepticism and ruthless denial of human worth. Polanyi affirms instead the creative personal role in knowledge as a way of understanding the rise of human life and as a clue to the story of evolution. While Camus's approach is through literature and Polanyi's through science, each presents an affirmative philosophy emphasizing powerfully the force of individuation in the processes of life.

Polanyi acknowledges the affinities between personal knowledge and the insights of pragmatism, existentialism, and phenomenology.[38] All of these philosophies have in this century highlighted in distinctive ways the contribution of the self to knowledge. While they point to the need for a correction, they are not comprehensive enough to provide an alternative conception of scientific knowing and knowing in general. It is this further creative step that makes Polanyi's philosophy timely and original.

These various examples of links between the new philosophy of Michael Polanyi and academic philosophical inquiry do show the prophetic quality of his thought. He anticipated and saw the direction that others are now moving toward. They also reveal some omissions in Polanyi's work. Polanyi could have been more like Wittgenstein and shown us the truth in positivism as well as its errors, the difference between faith within science and within religion, or considered moral inversion as a case of taking justice out of the stream of life and making it into an unattainable absolute, as Wittgenstein would say.[39] Or Polanyi could have made more explicit, as Ramsey prefers, the ontology of tacit knowing, and thereby avoided the misunderstanding of psychologism.[40] Such criticisms are important. But they do not diminish or deny the central thesis of Polanyi's work. Neither do they excuse the myopia of philosophers who move closer to Polanyi's position without acknowledging it or its importance. One such philosopher regards Polanyi as an obscurantist and yet himself labors to show the difficulty of exact and explicit definitions and operations in scientific knowledge.[41] Compared to these recently-dead and living philosophers, the work of Polanyi has not only parallel insights but also a towering relevance and comprehensiveness that is strikingly absent from the others. His thoughts are not primarily directed to or for the sake of other philosophers but to all the thinkers who are concerned about the destiny of our society. In this respect, Polanyi's grasp of our historical predicament and the relevance of his philosophy to it are carried much further.

PHILOSOPHY OF NATURAL AND SOCIAL SCIENCE

While academic philosophy has definitely advanced toward positions similar to Polanyi's, natural and social scientists are more pronounced in their recognition of the importance of this heuristic philosophy. Leonard K. Nash has developed a philosophy of "real" science, indicating as Polanyi does, that we need to catch science in action rather than depend upon the "ideal" science of philosophers.[42] Proceeding from his career in chemistry, Nash takes an approach based primarily upon actual events in the history of science and in the reflections of scientists themselves. Generous in his use of Polanyi's material, Nash perhaps comes closest to expressing their mutual concern for the objective ideal of knowledge as a misrepresentation of science when he says:

Speaking of self-sufficient Method—scientific, experimental, statistical, or what you will—we speak of a chimera. A Method, seeking to invest the construction of science with an inhuman certainty, must seek a dehumanization of science that ends inevitably by making science humanly impossible. Potential danger then lurks in the myth of Method—danger that working scientists might actually come to take it seriously. In the social sciences credulity of this myth exacts a heavy toll. . . .[43]

Like Polanyi, Nash recognizes in the fundamental structure of knowing the contribution of the individual. Speaking of the nature of perception, he says "seeing involves a merging of something from the object, 'outside,' with something contributed by the viewer, from inside."[44] Like Polanyi, Nash also stresses the importance of the premises of our language and of tradition in guiding us to discoveries, the necessity of skill in applying any rule or formalism, and the limitations of "concurrence" in determining scientific truth.[45] Such agreements between Nash and Polanyi lead to a similar view of the great turning points in the history of science as being ones that would be impossible if the popular conception of the scientific method were adhered to strictly.[46] Such support for a Polanyian view of science and knowledge is all the more striking when it is understood that Nash is contending that his account of natural science is based upon the largely-shared common understanding and practice of scientists.[47] If Nash is correct, as it seems he is, by his wide survey and quotation from the works of many scientists, Polanyi's philosophy speaks more accurately for the "real" scientists, and one has to take seriously the charge that the objective ideal of knowledge is a distortion dangerously at work in our culture.

Another natural scientist who applies the insights of Polanyi most extensively is William T. Scott.[48] Drawing upon his research in theoretical cloud physics, he gives a beautiful illustration of the epistemological and ontological personal involvement of the knower and the many-leveled structure of reality.[49] Study of clouds demands many of the principles given in Polanyi's philosophy. Clouds are studied in three scales of organization: microscale, tiny drops of water; mesoscale, immediate cloud region; and macroscale, air movements over continents and around the world.[50] The relating of these entities shows the Gestalt operations suggested in Polanyi's philosophy. For example, "comprehension at each level requires the recognition of organizing principles appropriate to the level, principles which cannot be derived from those governing subordinate levels."[51] Molecular processes of evaporation and condensation govern the rates of growth of water droplets at the microscale, but the dynamics and structure of the surrounding mesoscale clouds determine which particular circumstances for droplet growth will occur. Still, the mesoscale behavior of a cloud is dependent upon heat and evaporation, as well as upon the motion of large air masses in the region as determined by the macroscale.[52] Scott finds and demonstrates in detail how Polanyi's principles of marginal control and of a stratified universe are characteristic of atmospheric conditions, and ones that are also inherent in the nature of knowing. As Scott points out, no principles that can define a cloud can be derived from the microscale.[53] It is also impossible for the larger scales to define operations at the lower levels. The mesoscale while influencing conditions for droplet growth cannot define or determine, for instance, the principles of condensation of the water droplet.

Scott's confirmations of Polanyi's theory of knowledge in the work of theoretical cloud physics are shown in the role of tacit knowing in cloud identification, the necessity for personal guidance of computer programs in collecting and interpreting weather conditions, the indwelling involved in the use of meteorological tools and equations, the failure of the Laplacean ideal in cloud physics, the greater objectivity and value of a theory based upon Polanyi's model of personal knowledge compared to one based upon the objective ideal, the government and administration of cloud physics, and the necessary ultimate commitments and beliefs of such scientists.[54] For Scott, Polanyi provides a true and useful way to illuminate the "underlying assumptions and principles of research in the physics of precipitation."[55]

Besides these representative responses in chemistry and physics, scientists in the biological fields also show a discontent with the accepted philosophy of science and a turn toward the direction indicated by Polanyi.[56] Sir Francis Walshe states that our age has tended to develop mechanistic concepts of life and mind.[57] The two main factors that have led to this condition are first, the trend of thought since Galileo, and second, the electrical approach to the nervous system.[58] We have virtually abolished, says Walshe, the concept of the mind and have reduced it to physics and chemistry. Reviewing the history of modern neurophysiology, he shows that it is mainly analytical and reductionist and that both the critique and the alternative suggested by Polanyi are especially promising. The chiefly electrical approach of neurophysiology has the difficulty of studying parts without relation to the whole subject.[59] Little is yet known from this approach about how physiological states produce consciousness, and it has led to a series of absurdities and confusions.[60] After having denied the existence of the mind, the neurophysiologist continues to talk as if it existed.[61] Some researchers while trying to use a computer model for brain action keep saying "we," implying a knower and a doer, not a machine.[62] Walshe therefore concludes that such neurophysiology has failed to provide a feasible account of the brain-mind relationship.

Looking at neurobiology and the philosophy of Polanyi, Walshe suggests Polanyi's positive contributions. The ability to select what is interesting and illuminating is one of the characteristics that a machine does not share with the mind.[63] The biologist needs to understand that when dealing with living beings he or she must have a logic of achievement that is not a factor in the physical sciences. An achievement is subject to success or failure; in chemical processes there is neither.[64] Michael Polanyi also shows that biologists are accounting for the dynamic properties of living organisms in mechanistic terms, but the biologist's consciousness and actions are not explicable by these terms. No biblical fundamentalism could be more rigid, according to Walshe, than the demand that biology be only physics and chemistry.[65] Even though we may have to "fractionalize" to do experiments, we should not confuse methods with the comprehensive entity that we are seeking to understand. Polanyi's view of body and mind acknowledges the importance of the physiology of the person, but it does not reduce the mind to this.[66]

Even at the molecular level of biology, some biochemists, such as Arthur Peacocke, have seen the bearing of Polanyi's thought on

[123]

their work. Besides concurring with Polanyi that the existence of science requires a society which makes certain value judgments and that a Gestalt-like knowing is entailed in scientific experiment and observation, Peacocke sees Polanyi as providing a more precise and biochemically accurate way of speaking of the development of one form of life from another.[67] Following Polanyi's analysis of a machine's principles of engineering that cannot be reduced to physics and chemistry, Peacocke applies it to a living cell and the molecular structures that contribute to biological specificity. Speaking of the living cell, Peacocke says:

The argument has been worked out with reference to a machine but applies with even greater force and clarity to, say, a living cell, with its complex configuration in space and time, with its flow of constantly changing substances both within and across the cell membrane and with its possession of an individual 'life-cycle.'[68]

And in reference to the molecular structure of genetic material:

The chemical structure of DNA, the covalent and hydrogen bonds which link them, thereby enabling specific base-pairs (A-T, G-C) to be formed, are describable in terms of the categories of physics and chemistry and are studied on this basis by 'physical biochemists' and 'biophysicists.' However, the particular and unique sequence of base pairs ... that occurs in any DNA molecule present in the nuclei of the cells of a particular organism can never be explained by any purely chemical process. Chemical processes are, indeed, the means whereby bases are incorporated into chains of DNA but the sequence in which the bases are assembled in the DNA is a property of the whole organism.[69]

Thus, Polanyi's heuristic philosophy, which takes its clue from the way parts are integrated into wholes, opens up a new possibility for the understanding of emergence of forms of life without the introduction of terms alien to the scientific process.

Continuing our survey of Polanyian movements in the philosophy of science, two of the most pioneering figures in humanistic psychology, Abraham Maslow and Carl Rogers, have seen in Polanyi the breakthrough to an understanding of science congenial to the study of the person. Maslow speaks of Polanyi's work as "required reading for our generation," and Rogers asserts that the heart of the change now needed for a science of the person is summed up in the words of Polanyi.[70] Like Polanyi, Maslow sees the mechanistic assumptions of science as obstacles to adequate psychological study. Instead, there is a need for openness to other intellectual frameworks that go beyond the limitations of classical science. Classical science fails most clearly when we come to the higher reaches of human nature. Classical physics wisely ignores purposes, but human sciences cannot, as Polanyi has shown.[71] In a similar vein, Carl Rogers calls for a reexamination of the philosophy of the behavioral sciences. Rogers sees a continuing place for the rigor and the precision of science, but he argues that these must be set in a wider context of understanding.[72] Granting the value of other emphases such as the sociological, Rogers contends that in science we must give a primary value to the person because "only in the individual does awareness exist."[73] Science viewed from this angle is both more humanizing and more open to discovery. In a brief statement, Rogers and his colleague, William Coulson, summarize the new direction suggested by a fuller inclusion of the significance of the person:

. . . all of this which we have known as science becomes but one modest part of science. It can be seen as imbedded in an impressive personal context in which personal and group judgment of plausibility becomes as important as statistical significance. The model of a precise, beautifully built, and unassailable science (which most of us hold, consciously or unconsciously) becomes, then, a limited and distinctly human construction, incapable of precise perfection. Openness to experiences can be seen as being fully as important a characteristic of the scientist as the understanding of *research design. And the whole enterprise of science can be seen as but one portion of a larger field of knowledge in which truth is pursued in many equally meaningful ways, science being one of those ways.*[74]

The impact of such a view on the behavioral sciences would be, as Rogers states, to shift study away from what can be most easily measured to a fuller study of the many facets of human nature and to give a new dignity to the sciences of the person and to those who commit themselves to this field.[75]

In sociology and political science, there is also a movement in the same direction as Polanyi. Robert Bellah calls for a wider understanding of knowing as seen in Polanyi's work, a need to include the "cities of the interior."[76] In Bellah's view, we have concentrated too much upon the mastery of objects, which has led to our present fragmentation of reality. But, he believes, our realization of the inadequacy of this approach has already dawned, and that we are living in a post-modern and post-traditional society.

Comparing Polanyi and Max Weber, sociologist Raymond Aron sees Polanyi as "a philosopher of reconciliation, convinced that it is only through a misunderstanding of its true nature that science disenchants the universe," while he sees Weber as "a philosopher of contradiction dedicated to science, but in suffering, with the covert sorrow of being excluded by the progress of science from the paradise of faith."[77] Aron finds a mutual concern in the thought of Weber and Polanyi for the variety and uniqueness of human life, but a key difference in Weber's separation of fact and value and in Polanyi's denial of that possibility.[78]

Surveying Polanyi's thought, Aron finds five major propositions that contribute to a new theory of historical and sociological knowledge.[79] First, only the method of the creative scientist can reveal the nature of scientific knowledge. Second, it is unreasonable to sacrifice the interesting to the demonstrated since no scientific body of knowledge is wholly demonstrated. Third, any science becomes self-contradictory when it attributes a nature to its object that renders its own existence inexplicable or unintelligible. Fourth, all facts presuppose a framework of interpretation, and the framework is never refuted, demonstrated, or imposed by the facts themselves. Fifth, any proposition, whether in physics or in broader intellectual systems, is always subject to doubt and to revision. Such a set of propositions indicates the way in which Polanyi's thought moves from the separation of the experiment and the experimenter to an integral view of their connections in sociological and historical studies.

In political science, Bertrand de Jouvenel describes Polanyi's thought as having progressed "from a renovated conception of intellectual activity to a renovated image of man" that will have a pervading influence upon political philosophy."[80] He explores the idea of the republic of science on the Polanyian lines of a self-coordinated system of activities that sustains and regulates high professional standards. Such a view offers a rich possibility for the problem of political organization in which there is a need to find a way for creative endeavor and development. While science and society do not have the same specific goal, the government of science with its freedom and self-regulation suggests a model for a free society. "If so, just as the body scientific is a 'conspiration' for the dynamic unfolding of truth, the body politic would be a 'conspiration' for the dynamic unfolding of virtue."[81]

Carl Friedrich sees another innovation for political theory in Polanyi's thought, a new possibility for the discussion of natural law.[82] Even though Polanyi does not discuss natural law, his grounding of cultural values in a society with universal intent suggests a "natural-law theory in human nature."[83] The importance of this suggestion is that it overcomes the rigid and inflexible view of natural law as well as the relativistic and subjective view, both of which have made natural law untenable in recent history. Polanyi's sense of a reality that is continuously discovered and widened contributes to an understanding of higher laws which are capable of indefinite expression. It is not the content of natural law that changes, but our understanding of it. We cannot return to the old natural law of eternally valid principles, but we are driven to

[127]

find out what is right in our situation today. Recent international crimes that violate no explicit law have revived the importance of our understanding of natural law. By claiming that humans are moved by moral and intellectual passions with universal intent toward an inexhaustible reality and by showing that judgments, including judicial decisions, are integrations of particulars into comprehensive feats greater than their parts, Polanyi clears ground for a new conception of natural law. This concept of natural law would not contain the idea of explicit and eternal rules but rather a "situation sense" bearing upon transcendent aims and values. It would be a counterbalance to the absoluteness of both totalitarian and liberal regimes.

Finally, the history and philosophy of science as seen in the work of Thomas Kuhn show a major turn toward the direction of Polanyi's philosophy. Kuhn's work is now widely studied and accepted as a major insight into the nature of scientific advances and revolutions. Few notice, however, what Kuhn himself points out, namely, the affinity between his own notion of the centrality of a paradigm in scientific practice and Polanyi's demonstration of the role of a Gestalt-like framework of beliefs that shape and guide scientific discovery. At a 1961 symposium on "The Structure of Scientific Change" at Oxford University, Kuhn made this relation explicit in these words:

> . . . Mr. Polanyi himself has provided the most extensive and developed discussion I know of the aspect of science which led me to my apparently strange usage [of paradigm]. Mr. Polanyi repeatedly emphasizes the indispensable role played in research by what he calls the 'tacit component' of scientific knowledge. This is the inarticulate and perhaps inarticulable part of what the scientist brings to his research problem: it is the part learned not by precept but principally by example and practice.[84]

The popularity of Kuhn's thesis about paradigm changes indicates the extent to which the objective ideal of the progress of science, as expressed in the Baconian method, is dying. Even so,

Polanyi has discriminated between his position and that of Kuhn by insisting that we must go further than disproving the older objective ideal. We have to account for what it is in the nature of scientific knowing that leads the creative and original mind to hold to a new grasp of reality that appears at odds with the established paradigm.[85] There are no rules for this procedure. Only a new theory of knowledge in science that allows for the risk of failure and for the universal intent of the individual scientist provides for the grounds of such change. This new theory is what Polanyi calls personal knowledge and tacit knowing.

ART AND THEOLOGY

Other major areas in which Polanyi's thought is being pursued in parallel and collaborative lines are art and theology. A reader of Polanyi's philosophy soon becomes aware of its interdisciplinary character and particularly of its relating natural science to the humanistic fields. Art and religion are especially in the range of Polanyi's concern, and it is not surprising that scholars in these areas have seen the relevance of his thought and have begun to employ it.

In 1970, physiologist M. H. Pirenne published *Optics, Painting & Photography* in which he presented a major insight based on Polanyi's conception of tacit knowing, particularly the Gestalt integration of subsidiary awareness into focal awareness.[86] The import of Pirenne's work is to show that the ideal of "an artist wishing to hold a mirror to Nature" is a form of the objective ideal of knowledge and as such can remain only an unattainable ideal.[87] In his conclusion, Pirenne claims that, in principle, a representational painting contains some of the same kind of aesthetic elements as a purely "abstract" painting.[88] But the result of this idea is not to throw art into a sheer psychologism. Pirenne shows that the main characteristic of human vision has not changed in history.

What have changed are the methods and the subject. Such changes do not mean "that there are no permanent optical laws relating to human vision, and that the evolution of art must be explained entirely on subjective grounds...."[89] Pirenne notes that the work of Polanyi shows that it is our own subsidiary awareness of the flatness of the surface of a representational painting that prevents us from distorting it into a perception of actual flatness. Relying upon such awareness, we modify our vision and see within the painting its suggestion of depth and perspective. Such a modification is akin to our not mistaking a staged murder within a drama for an actual murder.[90] Our perceptions are a function of our background awareness, and this principle holds from representational to highly abstract painting.

In a similar way Polanyi connects our understanding in science through its theories of nature with the imagination of art. Returning to our earlier exposition of Polanyi's view of metaphor and art as "an integration of incompatibles," we can see at this point how this conception applies even to science. Just as a representational painting detaches and distorts elements in nature in order to give a view of reality, so do scientific theories that compare nature to a wave, a particle, or a machine. These, too, are integrations of incompatibles into creative perspectives that serve to guide us to a new depth of reality. They can only function with the background of our subsidiary awareness that gathers up from our indwelling of reality the clues that are focused in the frame and the story or the theory before us. Just as we do not mistake a painting or a play's murder for reality but see reality through this device, neither do we mistake a scientific theory for reality, but see reality through it.

Polanyi's relevance to artistic creativity has been noticed by Arthur Koestler and Donald L. Weismann.[91] Koestler extends Polanyi's work on the role of our subsidiary awareness in originality and discovery. He further explores the biological and prearticulate heritage of our psychology that prepares us for making discoveries. Koestler finds a heuristic impulse in our being and a structure of knowing similar to Polanyi's conception that guides the acts of creativity in science and art. Less technical and theoretical but more readable and illustrative than Polanyi's work, Koestler shows in his own way the absurdity of an ideal of knowledge based upon strict objectivism. Most important to our concern here is that the wide acclaim of Koestler's work is significant evidence of the appearance of a new direction in our understanding of knowledge in our society.

Donald Weismann tells us of the relevance of Polanyi to the creative artist in his own story about sitting down to write. He begins his account with a preface that quotes from Polanyi:

We start the pursuit of discovery by pouring ourselves into the subsidiary elements of a problem and we continue to spill ourselves into further clues as we advance further, so that we arrive at discovery fully committed to it as an aspect of reality. These choices create in us a new existence, which challenges others to transform themselves in its image. To this extent, then, 'existence precedes essence,' that is, it comes before the truth that we establish and make our own.[92]

The significance of what Polanyi says unfolds as Weismann describes his struggles to write in a kind of laboratory of his own making, a room about thirty kilometers from Mexico City.[93] His purpose is to write a book that is a story of self-discovery, a book most likely about himself. Then he begins to make the strategic yet uncertain and unforeseeable choices. Throughout, Weismann illustrates the interplay of a chosen purpose or problem and of the creative intuition and imagination that guide us. After a week of writing from three to four thousand words, he has only eight hundred that seem worth keeping. Yet, he is not even sure of this choice. True to Polanyi's understanding of the genuine explorer, Weismann goes out into the night wondering if he will spend the year "writing a day, destroying a day; then painting a day and destroying that, *ad infinitum.*"[94] When he returns to his house, and reads again the first eight hundred words, he at first thinks they are foolish, and wants to tear them up. After having a cup of tea and reading *La Prensa*, he picks them up again and decides that he really has begun. Weismann concludes:

> ... *that whatever the eight hundred words were moving toward lay in a circle all around them, and that I would find my way of extending them. And in the long meantime that extends from the long-ago room in Mexico to this very place and moment I can rejoice in the good existence that this search keeps making possible for me.*[95]

In the area of theology, Polanyi has one of his earliest supports and allies. This response stems in part from the theologian's appreciation of the fiduciary component in tacit knowing and the recognition of its kinship with the Augustinian principle that in order to know one must first believe. But Polanyi's thought is no comfortable ally for theological concerns despite the favor with which many theologians have treated it. The challenge of Polanyi's heuristic philosophy to theology catches it at two vulnerable points.[96] The first is theology's own involvement in the dichotomy of knowing and being that is so prevalent in our thought today. The second is Polanyi's belief in the centrality of discovery in all knowing. In Polanyi's terms, theology, like all fields of knowing, is obligated to an openness to growth and discovery that is fundamental to being human and to earnest concern for the ever-deepening knowledge of reality. Theology cannot be true to the nature of tacit knowing without a dynamic growth in its own field. Such a heuristic conception of knowing challenges the separation of theology from other fields by disputing a special ground of investigation.[97] It calls for a vast rethinking of the theological enterprise as an involvement in a common structure of knowing.

Prominent among the theologians early in recognizing the importance of Polanyi's thought is H. Richard Niebuhr. Niebuhr sees in Polanyi a "moral philosopher" who has taken responsibility for his knowledge and carefully reflected upon it in such a way that he illuminates for others the role of faith in science and in society.[98]

Niebuhr's evaluation was borne out at a conference of theologically-concerned scientists at Oxford University in 1965; they took the position that Polanyi's epistemology makes intelligible the nature and compatibility of the scientific method with Christian faith.[99] They saw that in the search for truth, whether in science or theology, there is a commitment of the person that transcends the subjective or objective alternative through his or her universal intent.

Thomas Langford, a thorough theological scholar of Polanyi's thought, sees in it a major twofold challenge to Christian theology.[100] Realizing that Polanyi's heuristic epistemology leads to a basic reorientation of our thinking and a new comprehension of reality, he sees theology challenged to perform an apologetic task and a dogmatic task. The apologetic task of theology is to work for the establishment of the new theory of knowledge in order to counter the distinction between scientific and humane thinking. A rectification of outlook is called for to overcome the habits of our divisive thought. Polanyi, according to Langford, reunites the heuristic vision of worship with other great intellectual systems, opening up new possibilities for understanding between science and religion. The dogmatic task, that is, the systematic formulation of a contemporary theology, is to recover the personal knowledge that inheres in theology as a confession of faith and to expound the Christian version of reality known in worship. Langford therefore finds grounds and inspiration for the basic purpose of theology in Polanyi's heuristic philosophy.[101]

Philosopher of religion Jerry Gill finds in Polanyi's concept of tacit knowing a rational basis that explains the possibility of religious knowledge.[102] Gill is aware of the existence of the claims of religious knowledge in his daily life, but he seeks to find the philosophical grounds for such knowledge. Given our understanding of knowing in modern philosophy, Gill finds the chief difficulty to be one isolated by Polanyi, the dualism in this epistemology of fact and value. Gill then proceeds to develop a functional view of language using insights of Wittgenstein, Austin, John Wisdom, and others. This functional view discloses two main concepts, "awareness and response," that indicate Polanyi's contribution to understanding the problem of religious knowledge. Gill says:

A sound view of language necessitates interpreting knowledge as a function of contextual, dimensional, and tacit awareness. Grasping meaning in language depends upon being tacitly aware of the various dimensions or forces which make up the context of any given statement. Thus knowledge is inextricably bound up with experiential awareness. In addition, a sound view of language necessitates interpreting knowledge as a function of purposeful, committed, and creative response. Grasping truth in language depends upon responding as a total person to experience. Thus knowledge is also inextricably bound up with integrated activity; that is, with being fully human. [103]

Besides showing the affinity between later linguistic philosophy and Polanyi's philosophy, Gill indicates how theology, as interpreter of the contents of religious language, can speak with models and metaphors that are not simply odd and meaningless but are in harmony with other forms of meaningful and valid discourse.

Another pioneering impact of Polanyi's heuristic philosophy upon Christian theology is seen in the recent work of Thomas F. Torrance.[104] Torrance takes the relation of science and theology as a major and central problem for Christian theology in our time. Using the work of Polanyi, Einstein, and others, he writes to show that this relationship is definitely a positive one. One of his most provocative claims is that theology, in its understanding of being, opens up a way to understanding reality already indicated by Einstein but still waiting to be more fully realized.[105] At this point, Torrance sees the contribution of Polanyi as especially significant, for Polanyi has shown that "far from being self-explanatory and self-sufficient the universe is characterized by boundary conditions that are and must be left open and indeterminate by its own internal relations."[106] The human person, from this point of view, is the boundary condition "in the structure of the space-time universe where it is open beyond itself, and where the mystery of

[134]

meaning is constantly disclosed."[107] Looked at in this way, theology has a role to play in science in keeping science open to the invisible and less tangible structures of the universe as well as to its more material and tangible features. Indeed, it is with an ability to apprehend greater imperceptible and intangible magnitudes that recent science has penetrated more deeply. There is a fundamental kinship between the wonder and awe of worship and the dialogue of science with the realities of the universe.

While Polanyi has stimulated new ways of thinking in theology, his efforts are also supported by an original and creative theologian, Bernard J. F. Lonergan, who has developed an epistemology close to Polanyi's. Lonergan, like Polanyi, has taken the heuristic aspect of knowledge as the central clue. His major work, *Insight: A Study of Human Understanding*, was published at almost the same time as Polanyi's work, indicating an independent convergence upon the central problem of our scientific outlook.[108] He draws upon the thought of past and present philosophers, contemporary mathematical and physical theory, statistical methods, and psychological and sociological research. He compares insight to the comprehension and solution of a detective's puzzle, an analogy used by Polanyi in 1946 for the process of scientific discovery.[109] Also with similarity to Polanyi, Lonergan calls this act of solving a problem and gaining knowledge "understanding."[110] A further parallel is seen in Lonergan's belief that if we see the importance of insight, this will confer "a basic yet startling unity on the whole field of human inquiry and human opinion." Like Polanyi, Lonergan seeks to catch knowing in action and to show how understanding the way we know "brings within a single perspective the insights of mathematicians, scientists, and men of common sense." The congruence of many of the themes and concepts of Lonergan and Polanyi is recognized by theologian Langdon Gilkey who pursues the same themes to show how the issues of ultimate concern appear within scientific knowing and discourse.[111]

Along with the similarities of the epistemology of Lonergan and Polanyi, there are also major differences. Lonergan speaks primarily to theologians; Polanyi addresses all reflective persons. Lonergan grasps a radically new view of knowledge but is less polemical and universal in his applications of it. Lonergan writes in the logical style of scholastic theology; Polanyi writes in a dramatic philosophical manner that shocks, startles, and arouses thought. Together, Polanyi and Lonergan both indicate a major new direction in theology by overthrowing epistemological dichotomies and focusing upon the heuristic dimension of knowing.

A FOCAL POINT FOR CHANGE

Many more persons and movements than can be covered here are pursuing the issues raised by Polanyi and there are also many parallel lines of inquiry. But no person or movement has so singularly grasped as has Polanyi the causal connections between the objective ideal of knowledge generated by the scientific outlook and the disasters of our century. Nor has anyone else seen with the breadth of his understanding the alternative conception of knowledge that can deliver us from our plight. The forces of "the new consciousness," as Harold Schilling has called it, are signs that a new paradigm is emerging.[112] Polanyi has contributed a substantial philosophy of knowledge that serves as a focal point for this change. The processes are those of reformation, of calling us to a newer and deeper understanding of our own traditions in science and in learning in general. The consequences are revolutionary. For the first time since the conquest by the objective ideal of knowledge, there promises to be a new objectivity, built not by the separation of science from the person, of knowing from being, or by the introduction of some *deus ex machina* or third force. From within the reality and the knowledge of science that we share, Polanyi has established first, the way we achieve our knowledge and then, how we move from that understanding to newer and greater levels of knowing. We, as the whole structure of tacit knowing shows, are the instruments of exploration in the universe. The acceptance of this responsibility is our most important choice.

[136]

vi. The Transformation of Imagination

HISTORY AND HOPE[1]

We noticed earlier that Polanyi had observed that the main influence of science upon us is not through technology but through the impact of science upon our imagination and world view.[2] The greatest and most shaking changes of the modern world have come about through the ways that we have come to believe and to think. We saw in Chapter I how Polanyi grasped the logic of destruction in this century. The leaders of moral inversion and nihilism were not guided by technology but by the scientific outlook. This outlook brought into an active force the ancient ideas of mechanism and skepticism with the drive for perfectionism. This combination, represented in the dogma of the objective ideal of knowledge, worked the greatest havoc upon our civilization.

In the current crisis of our culture there is a tendency to focus mainly upon technology instead of upon the scientific outlook as the source of our problems.[3] Indeed technology does and can imperil our future. Still, the control and the uses of technology are first of all matters related to our basic beliefs about the nature and meaning of life. If we do not come to grips with the shaping power of the mistaken scientific outlook upon our assumptions, it is likely that we shall repeat in new ways the catastrophes of the past.

A survey of the pressing problems of our time reveals the omnipresence of the scientific outlook and its dangers to our future. Behind nearly every issue stands the influence of the objective ideal of knowledge. Most obvious perhaps is the collapse of the mores of a civilized society. The prevalence of street crime, bombings, hijackings, and governmental deceit in the industrial nations discloses the power of nihilism at the very roots of our social fabric. A second and alarming aspect of our situation is our difficulty in transmitting the best of our norms and aspirations to the next generation. So shaken is the confidence of the new generation in the performance of their elders that they are reluctant to receive or to learn from them. Dropping out of school and revolting against science have become frequent forms of this breakdown. A third feature is our state of gloom and pessimism about the future. As a realistic view about our condition, such an attitude is valuable. When belief in our ability as a human race to cope with our affairs fails, this portends defeat. The gloom that hovers over us is our awareness of the limits of our capacities to plan and to engineer social change. The dashed hopes for progress in this century and the last one have disenchanted us from dreams of possible solutions. Finally, our problems are heightened by sheer physical discomfort and pain in a world environment that is rapidly deteriorating as we continue the pace of our production and consumption of industrial commodities. Growth of population, the depletion of natural resources, and economic instabilities intensify our ecological plight. We are suffering a "civilizational malaise," one that reflects the achievements of a scientifically-based culture unable to inspire and direct its destiny.[4]

At the center of this predicament is the human knower. Flight from science is neither a reasonable nor a desirable approach. The benefits of science are colossal. From within science we must find grounds for our hope and recovery. At this fundamental level, Polanyi's heuristic philosophy is most crucial. Through his reconceptualization of knowing according to the example of scientific discovery, he upholds science as a way of knowing in our future yet transforms its implications for understanding ourselves and our place in the universe.

A retrospective view of our preceding chapters offers at least five ways that Polanyi's philosophy re-presents science as at one with our human hopes. The first is the creative relationship between tradition and innovation.[5] On the one hand, his critique of unbridled perfectionism shows the danger of attempting to realize too quickly an inexhaustible ideal. On the other hand, tacit knowing of tradition explains the way great advances and breakthroughs occur that drastically alter and renew our insights into truth. The supposed necessity for conflict between tradition and free inquiry is changed into the rational yet passionate format of the controversies of science. The goal of progress requires neither the repudiation of all authority nor the condemnation of failure to attain cherished ideals as the result of hypocrisy. A great tradition provides the grounds for both its being maintained and its being changed. Thus, Polanyi's structure of tacit knowing demonstrates the relation between traditional frameworks, which form the background of our subsidiary awareness, and the acquisition of new knowledge, which is constituted from the present problems of our focal awareness.

A second principle of hope from within science is Polanyi's grasp of the knower's unity with the world. The process of indwelling in tacit knowing shows how we are constantly participating in the world, even when it seems at a distance from us. Our sense of separation is only the appearance of our focal knowledge as a distal term. As a structural process of all knowing, indwelling opens many possibilities for reinterpreting science and its relations to reality. Particularly important is the realization that the relations of science and nature are not inherently ones of alienation or of opposition but are relationships of communion and of integration.

A third way in which Polanyi's philosophy revitalizes science and hope is his joining human creativity in science with all the other arts of humanity. Everywhere, whether in the strict measurements and controls of physical science or in the painting of a masterwork, playfulness, guesses, and hints are combined with the trained and skilful performance that marks fruitful innovation. Creativity is not a choice between venture and a systematic approach. The paradigm of impersonal objective knowledge in science as one that guarantees certainty without reliance upon our passions or without the taking of risks is false. Originality in science, as well as in the arts, involves letting our imagination run free. The contributions of play, of laughter, of dancing, of celebration, of serendipity, of our whole selves are central to all forms of knowing.

Fourth, Polanyi's philosophy strengthens our unity with the world and with each other by its holistic and dynamic view of knowing. Instead of an attack upon specialization and the consequent fragmentation of knowledge, Polanyi attacks the assumption that such specialization and division of labor inevitably leads to misunderstanding and loss of common goals and values. The conception of knowing as having a common structure across the disciplines reveals a shared ground of understanding. This ground is the centrality of the person as the point of the intelligent integration of clues from the various facets of reality. By his concepts of boundary conditions and marginal control, Polanyi shows a view of the human knower emerging within the framework of evolution. This conception does not introduce the alien explanation of vitalism nor does it reduce human behavior to the overly simple view of mechanism. There is an ascent of potential human thought in Polanyi's picture of the rise of life. From lower physical and chemical conditions, new opportunities for higher principles to harness these conditions have occurred. There is no predetermined course that insists that these new principles will make good. With the flowering of human thought, there is the chance to know with a universal intent and also with the risk of failure.

Finally, Polanyi's heuristic philosophy, summarized in his image of a Society of Explorers, contradicts the concept of science as a neutral enterprise and leads to a view of history as a drama of moral purpose. In common with the beauty, elegance, and interest that motivate the most abstract and seemingly detached sciences and the practical concerns of politics for freedom, justice, and peace is the recognition that all knowers are personally involved beings. Progress in physics or in government does not come from objective conquest and detachment from events but comes from a giving of oneself to levels of reality that ever seek to manifest themselves in newer and deeper ways. Knowledge, whether in the routine applications of previous achievements or in the creative discovery of new frontiers, is always an act of human responsibility.

AN END TO DICHOTOMIES

Standing in the way of the transformation of our imagination are deeply ingrained habits of thought that shape and form the modern mind. The objective ideal of knowledge is propagated and renewed through the philosophies of knowledge that continue to foster schisms between mind and body, between reason and experience, between facts and values, or, in short, between the knower and the known. This epistemological dualism is the citadel of the objective ideal of knowledge. Our final step in appreciating the achievement of Michael Polanyi is to examine briefly this dualism in our knowledge and how Polanyi has convincingly overcome it.[6]

The greatness of Greek thought was its development of the tools for what Polanyi calls focal awareness. It introduced the importance of our reasoning faculties and the questioning of the world. More significant, it produced the basic polarity of our Western consciousness, the awareness of a thinking center and of a world to be understood. The concentration upon understanding the world and our methods of knowing it led to the possibility of objectivity and universality. But it also led to the tendency to bifurcate reality, to pose knowledge in terms of opposites, such as opinion and knowledge, or appearance and reality. While Polanyi does not offer an extensive review of our history of thought, his philosophy suggests major alterations in our interpretation of it. The great problem of our knowledge now is not so much the recognition of the importance of reason and of experience as it is the dichotomizing of the knower and the known and the denigration of the knower at the expense of the known. Greek thought excels in bringing to us one part of knowledge, the area of focal awareness or explicit knowing. What it introduced continues in modern science into a greater rift that we are now beginning to overcome, the separation of knowing and being.

Polanyi's philosophy began in opposition to one consequence of the great rift between knowing and being, the objective ideal of knowledge. In his examination of the nature of knowing itself, he came to a new view of knowledge that understands the importance of the focal target without divorcing it from the subsidiary particulars that contribute to it or from the person who integrates and indwells these to form knowledge. In so doing, he ends the need for dichotomies not only in scientific knowledge but in all forms of knowing.

The two greatest philosophers of the ancient world, Plato and Aristotle, and the founder of modern philosophy, Descartes, have similar concepts of knowledge as "final, impersonal and certain."[7] Plato projected a knowledge founded upon the certainties of eternity, above the change and flux of life. He sought a superior knowledge, one above the finitude of human beings. Aristotle found certainty within the world by emphasizing the order that was already there. He concentrated upon an analysis of the given data. Descartes established certainty independent of either a reality beyond the world or of a structure in the external world, by stressing the certainty of the rational and indubitable "idea" within the self. This emphasized our inner consciousness as our thinking center. But for all three, as Marjorie Grene demonstrates, the price of certainty was a conception of knowledge without genuine discovery and creativity, without true advance and novelty. For Plato, knowledge was recollection of truths already there in the world of eternal forms. Even with Aristotle's attention to the world of here and now, there was no place for discovery. His concern was for an analysis and articulation of an order already there. This was one reason why Aristotle's method had to be rejected in order for modern science to progress. The certainty of Aristotle's induction and observation contrasts sharply with the induction of modern science, which is never final and certain.[8] Descartes' method likewise departs from the actual practice and history of scientific discovery. Through his mathematical ideal of knowledge, he established a dualism of body and mind for modern philosophy and a belief in lucidity as the hallmark of knowledge. No fact of science nor any process of discovery achieves this kind of certainty, and if such certainty were actually followed, the method would inhibit scientific advance.[9] Besides the uniform stagnation of discovery inherent in the methods of these philosophical giants, their theories are strikingly characterized by the absence of a unique and knowing individual. In all three philosophies, knowledge is independent of the person and is the same everywhere because reason is alike in all persons.

Beginning with Galileo, modern science shifted the attention of philosophy to experience and observation and away from its rationalistic heritage, but philosophy did not turn to the nature of discovery, and so it continued the dichotomy of knowing in a search for valid knowledge. With Hume, this quest became skeptical since a knowledge based mainly on the senses could afford no certainty. Hume found our knowledge to be based upon our association of sense impressions through habits and custom. Intrinsically, there was no reason other than habit itself for believing this to be knowledge, and there was no knower except for the cognizing center of a bundle of impressions.[10]

Kant perceived the predicament of Hume's analysis, namely, that things out there do not simply get themselves known without a knower.[11] Kant saw that the receptivity of the mind to sense impressions is not enough to account for knowledge. He reversed the epistemological relations by centering the world around the knower instead of the knower around the world, and he separated the realm of natural knowledge from moral knowledge by his distinction between the phenomenal and the noumenal. Together these approaches seemed to Kant to provide an understanding of how the mind by its constructive work contributed to the certainty of science.

While Kant answered Hume by showing that without a theory of the mind we cannot account for the subjective unity of experience or for experience itself, he bequeathed to us some of the most serious dichotomies of our modern intellectual situation. One is the divorce between the knowledge of science and the knowledge of morality and religion. Another is that his knower, though an active agent, is empty and lacking individuality. The mind is a center organizing through categories but it is devoid of the features of human activity "born somewhere at some time of some parents, possessing some innate aptitudes, moulded somehow by the setting of his family, society, time."[12] This lack of historical and individual character in Kant's knower was founded upon his acceptance of the Cartesian dualism of thinking of mind as set against dead nature. It is a conception of knowledge based upon the exact, mathematized knowledge of the inorganic world. The consequence of Kant's momentous work was finally to produce a theory very much at home in the world of Newton but unable to tell us about living things.

While such a theory might appear to settle many problems, we are forced to see eventually that a theory of knowledge that does not tell us about living things, especially such as persons, is grossly inadequate. This consequence is one aspect of our present predicament, one that underlies our futile belief in the objective ideal. It is the culmination of what Schrödinger indicated as the "exclusion principle," the attempt to give an account of reality without an inclusion of the conscious personality that knows the reality claimed.[13]

The thread of this story in philosophy is suggested here. The yawning chasm of dualism in our knowing has persisted in many ways and is present even among some of the strongest philosophical revolts against the objectivism of science, such as existential-ism. Reacting against the external and impersonal domination of our world, Sartre, for example, has attempted to face with honesty the consequences of our common crisis by accepting within the subjectivity of the self the whole burden of knowledge.[14] Ultimately, this courageous attempt fails because of the isolation of the self that springs from Sartre's Cartesian dualism of mind and body. Polanyi has put this most clearly in his general criticism of existentialism for trying to build up knowledge from ground zero.[15] On the other hand, logical positivism has also reacted against objectivism in science by retreating to the position that scientific statements, instead of being about reality, are statements about sense data. Instead of having statements that are upheld as true, we obtain statements that can be "verified" by tracing them to the sense data on which they are based. Logical positivism's reaction is an attempt to save the objective ideal by reducing objectivity to that which has a lack of depth or of ultimacy.

When one looks back over even this cursory history of philoso-phy, it becomes clearer why our views of knowledge have produced the objective ideal. The emphasis generally has been upon securing the permanence and certainty of knowledge, an aim that has given rigor and clarity to human achievement. The concern for the creative process within knowledge has been neglected in favor of the certification of the already known. We have observed here the absence of a place for discovery, of individuality, of living things, and of persons in these philosophies. It is therefore not surprising that we have problems in our mode of knowing today that restrict and threaten human existence.

Polanyi's overcoming of a dichotomized or dualistic form of knowing can be seen further in three current intellectual issues that beset our general out ook: 1) the separation of fact from value, 2) the reduction of living things to mere physics and chemistry, and 3) the meaninglessness of persons. Each of these is a consequence of our deeply ingrained split between the knower and the known.

The fact and value separation is notorious, but it has received a shallow treatment.[16] Almost any enlightened person admits to the impossibility of being completely unbiased and intends to guard against the danger of being biased. But this attitude supports the belief in the objective ideal of knowledge; it does not really expose its falseness. The misleading basic assumption here is that there really are facts that are objective if we can remove human bias. This suggests that the human contribution to knowing is its defect and that the more we can remove this human element, the truer and more factual our knowledge will be. A second flaw follows from this position, namely, that values are subjective and are mere conventions without ultimacy; thus, a belief in only facts as strictly objective makes all other appraisals inferior to facts because they lack the same status.

The heuristic philosophy of Polanyi attacks directly this fact and value separation. In Polanyi's view there can be no purely factual statements.[17] All intelligent statements presuppose evaluation and judgment. Interest, belief, and appraisal are essential to the finding and holding of what we claim to be factual or true. All factual statements assume a Gestalt-like and fiduciary background integrated by personal acts of judgment and built upon clues within our subsidiary awareness. When this tacit structure is ignored and values are regarded as inferior to facts, we also lessen our humanity. The highest standards allow humans to become the highest persons. To deny people these standards is to limit not only their rights, but their humanity.[18]

A second current issue that stems from the epistemological dualism of objectivism and that affects the future of humanity is the attempt to reduce living things to mere physics and chemistry. This attempt ranges from the mechanistic models of human behavior such as those of B. F. Skinner and José Delgado to the works of molecular biologists, such as Francis Crick and Jacques Monod.[19] The consistently destructive element in this view is that it denies the character of life itself as well as life's various levels and forms. Life is seen to be ultimately a highly complex machine explainable entirely in the terms of physics and chemistry.

The errors of this reductionist position are now being more critically discussed.[20] Polanyi's critique is among the most acute

[146]

and also one of the few to offer a major conceptual alternative. The reductionist error follows from the objective ideal that took the materialism and exactness of physics and chemistry as the model of scientific explanation. This ideal, represented in the Laplacean belief that a complete atomic knowledge of the world would give us complete knowledge, is manifested in the contemporary belief that the real is the biochemical topography that constitutes organisms. Darwin's use of natural selection enhanced this attitude toward life by seeing life as the blind operation of chance and necessity, a paraphrase of mechanical forces. As a "teleology decapitated," to use Marjorie Grene's phrase, Darwinism served as a model of a one-level world.[21]

We have come in this last part of the twentieth century to an absurd position, where many are concerned about the preservation of life, while we have at large an understanding that equates living persons with complex biochemical machines. Before we can expect from science and government the kind of respect for and understanding of life that are necessary, we have to have in operation a mode of knowing that can acknowledge the distinctive character of living things. Polanyi's conception of hierarchy in the structure of tacit knowing provides this alternative. Through the concepts of boundary conditions and marginal control, he has shown how physics and chemistry provide conditions for life but leave open areas for the operation of new principles and the emergence of life.[22]

The problems of the fact-value dichotomy and the reduction of living things to physics and chemistry, besides being pervasive issues themselves, also point to the third example of destructive epistemological dualism in our society. This problem appears in our need for a science of persons. As our mode of knowing has denied the valuing nature inherent in our being and has lacked a conception of reality rich and varied enough to include the multi-levels of life, it has failed even more to provide a basis for understanding human personality in its depth and fullness. One aspect of this failure appears in the understanding of human consciousness.

The reductionist tendency led to a denial of the reality of human consciousness itself and saw it as a disguised name for the neural operations of the brain. This concentration upon the central nervous system combined conveniently with the development of cybernetics and computers. The construction of artificial intelligence machines simulating human judgment seemed to give convincing proof of the reductionist position. Significantly, the proponents of this view overlooked the distinctive differences between human personality and "thinking" machines. If we ponder, as Polanyi suggests, the situation of the world if all machines should suddenly stop because of their destruction, we can see immediately a clue to the vast differences between human beings and machines.[23] The capacity to invent, to create, and to discover again and rebuild the world could only be done by persons. Thinking machines, while able to function in a binary system with an efficiency that humans cannot duplicate, are nevertheless limited in their scope. They cannot indwell the world, imagine, or intuit new dimensions of reality. By nature, they are limited to explicit inferences, to knowledge based upon premises already given.

Polanyi effectively shows the mistake in comparing human and machine knowing.[24] His heuristic philosophy of knowledge also undergirds the growing attempts to develop a science of persons. Abraham Maslow and Carl Rogers have both led in this movement and recognize the importance of Polanyi's contribution.[25] In order to have a science of persons that includes the affective domain as well as the cognitive, that recognizes the way feelings play an important part in significant discoveries, that understands the way institutions are for persons, that upholds human freedom as consistent with an existence built up from natural laws, and that allows for human purposiveness, we have to reject the dualistic kind of view that denies reality and unity to these aspects of life. Through his study of knowledge as an intellectual and personal commitment based upon the structure of tacit knowing, Polanyi gives the foundation required.

Knowledge is the achievement of persons. The processes of knowing in persons transcend the mere world of tangible features by the extension of our powers to receive clues subsidiarily. We integrate these clues into the ideas and standards which we can choose or not choose to follow, according to our personal judgment of their truth and value. As Eugene Wigner has pointed out, it is not enough to describe the purpose of our evolutionary adaptation as only the survival of ourselves and of our progeny. There are also "adaptations to surroundings to satisfy other desires, such as curiosity, understanding, what are usually called the higher purposes of life. . . . Man doesn't live by bread alone, so to speak, and not even if we add the bread of his progeny."[26]

To respond to the crisis of our culture as full human persons calls for a transformation of our understanding. Until the dichotomies of our thought are overcome by a new philosophy that unites our knowing and being, we shall remain alien to ourselves and our world. Polanyi's philosophy is a forerunner in the making of a new paradigm that offers us this integration. Along with others working independently, as well as with those using his thought, there is here the possibility of a rebirth of hope through a new vision of our history and purpose in the universe, which leads us to our concluding discussion.

THE MEANING OF HUMANITY

The issues of ethics, of moral purpose and standards, are ever-present in Polanyi's philosophy. His search for a new epistemology is never remote from the overwhelming issues of our time. But the sound of his moral concern is distinctive among the many voices of alarm that call for action. Instead of accusing us of a lack of moral fervor, Polanyi warns us that our unparalleled moral zeal in the modern world has contributed directly to our destructiveness. The drive for moral perfection, which has swept over the globe, has given us a passion for moral progress based upon the scientific outlook, and that has led to totalitarian regimes and individual nihilism. For this reason, Polanyi expresses great concern about our belief in our morality and ideals. Traditional values and beliefs that have guided and restrained us are denied, then disguised as scientific absolutes according to the strident logic of the objective ideal. Thus, we have moral inversion, the dynamo-objective coupling of moral passions denied according to scientific skepticism yet active in the assertion of ideologies and principles as scientific facts. This development has brought humanity to what Polanyi has called "a suffocating" misconception of the universe. On the one hand, we are denied the legitimacy of our moral aspirations. On the other hand, we are asked to be loyal to observed scientific findings. The basis for this loyalty or for the reformation of the findings in new discoveries cannot be adequately derived from the findings themselves since they do not allow for a belief in the truth and reality that transcend their own materialism.

The restoration of our hope lies in seeing meaning for humanity in a universe where what we believe to be true might turn out to be false.[27] The scientific outlook imbued with the objective ideal has led to an absurd view of the universe because it has tried to know without having a place for the risks and the faith of the knower who is at the center of this inquiry. The solution tendered by Polanyi, surprisingly, does not lead to a Promethean defiance of science or our knowledge of the structure of the universe. Instead, it leads to a conception of human knowing within the limitations of our evolutionary development and prospects. This evolutionary process has equipped us with the capacity to know in the extensive and imaginative ways of articulate thought and symbolization. Yet, we cannot know noncommittally. All knowing involves indwelling and participation in subsidiary ways that require our being a-critical. For humanity as a whole, the best of our knowing is an investment of ourselves in a long history that conceivably could turn out to be wrong.

The fear and pessimism that could come from this realization do not arise in Polanyi's thought because he follows the example of scientific discovery. Seen through this paradigm, we are given hope for our future instead of trembling desperation. Scientific discovery is a case of being responsible for reaching a perfection beyond one's own powers, yet having a hope of succeeding. Science seeks to know reality, a reality with the richness to disclose itself in continuing new ways in the future. Scientific work, having made the disciplined effort to know, instead of being crushed by the burden it undertakes, moves ahead by making itself so that it receives the help of reality.

This process of giving ourselves up to a difficult task and finding that by pouring ourselves into it we are met with a solution that satisfies and exceeds our expectations is one that has a religious analogy. Polanyi observes that there is a parallel between the process of scientific discovery and the Pauline scheme of redemption.[28] As the Christian is set with the obligation to pursue an unattainable perfection and yet by the act of faith is aided by grace to have what is beyond his or her powers, the scientist by surrendering his or her efforts to a good problem is visited by the understanding that seems beyond realization.

The point of Polanyi's comparison is not a plea for particular religious beliefs. His concern is for the recovery of an understanding of humanity that can face its responsibility to seek the truth even when the enterprise seems to be one that is impossible or could be mistaken. Doubt and skepticism, instead of being expurgated from knowing, have to be included in a wider framework of understanding. To know does entail a fiduciary framework, such as forms of commitment. Since belief is inherent in knowing, so also is doubt. These components of belief and of doubt do not undermine the process that leads to discovery and the acquisition of knowledge. Once this fact becomes understood, it may be that religion itself will be transformed by the new situation and will speak meaningfully to humanity again.[29]

The problem before humanity now, however, is not the problem of religion. It is the problem of a type of historical consciousness and of authority. The scientific outlook and the objective ideal of knowledge have created a consciousness in modern humanity that is less able to experience and to enter into the venture of the highest ideals in the face of risk. The authority of the objective ideal of knowledge to discount values and beliefs that cannot be materially proven limits our sense of reality. This authority reduces existence to the calculus of mechanics and a one level ontology.[30] Consequently, humanity's prospects are bleak until it can resume a view of the universe as a place that offers meaning only through the responsibilities and the hazards of personal knowledge.

The problem of our historical consciousness and the nature of authority in defining knowledge and reality is illustrated in Polanyi's discussion of the Hungarian Revolution of 1956. This rebellion was more than one of force and of economic interests. The Hungarian Revolution was an uprising in the name of truth and of morality, causes so alien to our established scientific outlook that even major Western commentators failed to grasp their significance. Seeing reality from a different point of view, Polanyi opened our eyes to this event as a major turning point in our history.[31]

True to his emphasis upon the example of scientific discovery, Polanyi in looking at the revolution asked why people who were leaders and held major positions in the Communist party should suddenly change to a new point of view. The objectivist interpretation offers the explanation that increased industrialization made the oppressive tactics of Stalinism no longer necessary. No evidence is able to support this claim satisfactorily, but the claim is readily accepted because it fits the established outlook. This case is similar to the textbook explanation of the genesis of Einstein's theory of relativity, where it was long held to have begun with a discrepancy in the Michelson-Morely experiment instead of recognizing the theoretical genius of Einstein's imagination.[32] The claim that change in Hungary occurred because of increased industrial productivity does not deal with the contradiction that two of the most industrialized Communist countries of Eastern Europe, Czechoslovakia and East Germany, were also among the most repressive governments remaining.

The events that led to the Hungarian rebellion were a three-stage historical progression of revolt against government rule by lying and deception; it was a struggle to return to the independent power of truth in public life.[33]

The first stage of the revolt began when leading Western intellectuals abandoned "the God that failed" in the late 1930's as a result of the ruthless tactics of Stalin. By the end of the Second World War, there was an ardent group of former Communists critical of Communism's contradictions and failures.

The second stage reached its climax on the day Stalin died. Immediately thirteen Kremlin doctors, under sentence to death on their own false confessions, were released. This action signaled a turn to a preference for truth. Soon, at the Twentieth Party Congress in 1956, further revelations of Stalin's atrocities led to the denouncing of his regime, and new foundations for government were begun.

Four months after the Twentieth Party Congress, the third stage of these events began with a demand for reform and freedom of expression in the Petöfi Circle in Hungary. The Petöfi Circle was an official organ of the Communists led by trusted members of the Party. There the Marxist-Leninist doctrine was challenged by the members, and in its place an affirmation was made of the importance of a free press, rule by law, and the independence of the arts from subservience to the state. It was this change that produced the central opposition that later overthrew the government of Hungary. That this intellectual avant-garde spoke for the aspirations of the people became evident as the people came out into the street and the army gave them its support.

Despite this progression of public events leading to the Hungarian Revolution, major current political theory found it difficult to recognize the role of the desire for truth and independence of thought. Polanyi exposes here the captivity of our consciousness and its denials of the power of truth and ideals to transform our lives with two striking examples, the comments of a Soviet expert and the outlook of a political science textbook. First, Polanyi quotes the account of Richard Pipes, then Associate Director of Harvard's Russian Research Center, who, following the Twentieth Party Congress and the Hungarian Revolution, planned to say in a scholarly article that "the modern Russian intellectual had a very special mission to fulfill: 'to fight for truth.' "[34] On the advice of friends, Pipes omitted this passage because "it sounded naïve and unscientific." In 1964, four years after his article was published,

[153]

Pipes published another article asserting the importance of the struggle for truth and his regret that he had omitted the passage because "truth" did not fit the generally accepted explanations of his science.

In the second example, from a major political science textbook, the author takes the position that only events that can be observed by the senses are proper subjects of inquiry.[35] Such a position deliberately eschews value statements and scorns a question such as "What is a good society?" Confronted with the changes in beliefs of the intellectuals that inspired the Hungarian Revolution, this political science approach is unable to include the most crucial factors. For example, writing in October 1956 just a few weeks before the outbreak, Miklos Gimes spoke of how the Hungarian Communists had lost their way:

Slowly we had come to believe . . . that there are two kinds of truth, that the truth of the Party and the people can be different and can be more important than the objective truth and that truth and political expediency are in fact identical. . . . And so we arrived at the outlook . . . which poisoned our whole public life, penetrated the remotest corners of our thinking, obscured our vision, paralyzed our critical faculties and finally rendered many of us incapable of simply sensing or apprehending truth. This is how it was, it is no use denying it.[36]

An objective political science can observe that a change of outlook did occur and can even regard it as an intellectual triumph for having moved from one position to another. Yet, it cannot account in such a change for the decisive role of personal knowledge seeking truth, nor can it understand that the comprehensive outlook was not overthrown by direct objective argument or observation. The change in outlook was "a smashing of spectacles" through which they saw. Such changes were not made merely to have one view of reality instead of another but because of a belief in the truthfulness of one view over the other.

The lessons of the Hungarian Revolution transcend the issues of rival political and economic systems. The message discerned by Polanyi pertains to our understanding of how we shape our destiny, to whether our knowing is necessarily a moral action. The attempt to view history without recognition of the central importance of values in human motivation leaves us without a full knowledge of reality. Until the personal pursuit of truth and the risk of knowing it can resume their place within the nature of knowing and especially scientific knowing, we are diminished in our capacity to explore and find our way.

In Chapter IV, we saw that Polanyi sees our knowing emerging within the logic of evolution. This long development is one in which successive levels of the organization of matter have afforded opportunities for the appearance of new levels of reality. Polanyi describes this process as one of dual control where a lower level sets boundary conditions that are open to being harnessed by marginal principles above them. He uses an elementary example of the art of building and its hierarchical character. It begins with the physics and chemistry of the materials themselves. The physics and chemistry of the materials give boundary conditions that are harnessed by technology, which in turn are boundary conditions harnessed by the architect, and so on to the building of a community. This analogy to the process of evolution illustrates the way human thought and responsibility emerge. That our knowing is rooted in matter and our thoughts are bodily thoughts is affirmed. It is also shown that the bodily roots of our thought are boundary conditions that leave open the possibility of our being guided by a new level of reality, the ideals and standards of civilization.

This evolutionary view of the emergence of human thought and of culture is consistent with the structure of our knowing how to make discoveries and to learn skills. By relying upon previous conditions in our subsidiary awareness, we are able to be open to the hopes and intimations of our focal awareness for a more universal and profound grasp of reality. We assume our powers of thought and action then in a heritage of evolution that has come to include history, culture, and tradition. This background affords us the platform from which we are launched continually into follow-

[155]

ing the expanding horizons of reality. Since we follow standards and hopes that we and our society have set for ourselves as we have gleaned hints of the way to journey, we are challenged with the responsibility to go with universal intent. The depth of reality exceeds our complete grasp, yet it beckons us forward by stages.

The task and meaning of humanity set forth by Polanyi are seen best when viewed against the time perspective of our evolutionary story. A scale of comparison suggested by G. M. McKinley presents this time perspective dramatically.[37] Taking the age of the earth as about two billion years and representing it on the scale of a calendar year, one day represents about 5,500,000 years of terrestrial history and one second about sixty-five years. Viewed from this standpoint, the bare earth begins on January 1, in February life begins with self-replicating molecules, unicellular organisms appear in April, and primitive invertebrates in May. In summer the land plants emerge, followed in the fall by the large reptiles, birds, and brainy mammals. "Man," equipped with sensitive hands, does not appear until December 31 and then only four hours before midnight. A few hours later, he makes beginning efforts at social life, but it is not until the last minute of the year that his first civilization is organized. The period of the founding of the great world religions occurs at about half a minute, then modern science at five seconds, and twentieth-century science barely half a second before midnight. Thus seen, the appearance of human thought and culture is a recent cosmic event. While humanity's continuing its groping for wider ranges of truth is hazardous and presumes patience, the perspective of time suggests that we are only at the dawn of its flowering in the pursuit of truth.

In the twentieth century, we have reaped the destructive fruits of trying to make our knowing completely explicit and objective, ending in an absurd denial of the very structure of our own being as persons, and as a society. While this intensification of violence is in itself an urgent warning and a plea for a change in our direction, it is also a lesson in the capacities we have to plan and to guide social change. The ideals of modern civilization born from the rational hopes of scientific understanding are longer-ranged goals than we had understood. The belief in progress, the desire for liberty, equality, fraternity, are intimations of a potential reality deeper than we saw. They are goals worthy of a society of free and independent knowers, but they are complex goals exceeding the system of any group of persons. A new vision of a better society will preserve and reconceive these goals as ones to be pursued, but it will do so granting them the same range and indeterminateness that we face in the nature of scientific discoveries.

We have also learned more clearly in the twentieth century that nature is not an object; it is our home. We are a part of a larger whole whose unity and variety are still unfolding. Our capabilities of knowing and of forming a civilization have emerged within this natural process. We know not by actual separation from but by participation in myriad clues given through the unspoken realms of our being. For each level of our articulate thought there are virtually numberless levels supporting, guiding, and shaping it.

We have also learned in this century more about the role of beliefs in our knowledge. We cannot know without believing, at least in the rudimentary sense of what Polanyi calls subsidiary awareness and relying on. Indeed we are modified, changed, and directed by the outcomes of our beliefs. Consequently, there is a growth and transformation of our beliefs and also of our knowledge. These changes are made with a hunger for truth, for contact with a reality that is more universal, more satisfying to our total selves and history.

Such lessons rise from the heuristic philosophy of Michael Polanyi. Scientific discovery, instead of expunging our personal beliefs and our participation in the major task of knowing and shaping our planetary destiny, calls us to resume the pursuit of truth inexhaustibly. The meaning of humanity is, as Polanyi says for himself, "to seek the truth and to state our findings."

This calling places upon us an enormous responsibility to join with a Society of Explorers in a venture that is endless and hazardous. Viewed from the analysis of the structure of knowing as we break out and make new discoveries, we can assume our responsibility with the confidence that what we do is encouraged by the character of being itself.

The acceptance of this choice, the response to what appears as the invitation of the cosmos, remains, however, a tacit feat of comprehension that is like faith. It is the integration of particulars into a comprehensive understanding. It is a grasp of parts into a whole where the parts are present, but the whole means much more than its parts.

Such choices deserve and require the preparation of ourselves by the order and discipline of all achieved knowledge. The assimilation of what has gone before is a step of trust, albeit seemingly safe when others have already performed the feat. The step to discovery or the step to a new paradigm of knowledge is an inherently and intensely personal risking of ourselves in the vast human enterprise.

The challenge of our situation, the difficulties and the promise that it offers, is perhaps made clear in an incident in Polanyi's life. Some have ridiculed and others have admired a man who gave up a brilliant career in physical chemistry to turn to philosophy and the grave problems of our era. One day a friend, appreciative of his costly and difficult task, wrote to him the following lines from a monastic inscription in Latin:

In direst need he broke his cloister vows;
The hardest task is only done by him who cannot help it.[38]

NOTES

Introduction

1. Michael Polanyi, *The Tacit Dimension* (Garden City: Doubleday, 1966), p. 91.

2. Bronislaw Malinowski, "Culture," *Encyclopedia of the Social Sciences,* ed. Edwin R. A. Seligman (1937), 2, pp. 621-45.

3. Albert Camus, *The Myth of Sisyphus* (New York: Vintage Books, 1965).

4. Robert N. Bellah, ed. *Religion and Progress in Modern Asia* (New York: The Free Press, 1965), represents in variety the many ways the scientific outlook has affected this area.

5. "Upon First Sitting Down To Read *Personal Knowledge . . .*" in *Intellect and Hope,* eds. Thomas A. Langford and William H. Poteat (Durham: Duke University Press, 1968), pp. 3-18, gives an excellent account of the difficulties and unique demands upon the reader of Polanyi's thought. It suggests the almost total reorientation involved and the reflexive joys of this new perspective.

6. May Brodbeck, "A Review of *Personal Knowledge* by Michael Polanyi," *American Sociological Review,* 25 (August 1960), p. 583.

7. P. M. C. Davies, "Review of *The Logic of Personal Knowledge,*" *Philosophical Studies,* 28 (1969), p. 201.

8. Stephen Toulmin, "Review of *Personal Knowledge,*" *The Universities Quarterly,* 13 (1959), pp. 212-16.

9. Michael Polanyi, *Personal Knowledge: Towards a Post-Critical Philosophy* (Chicago: University of Chicago Press, 1958), chap. I.

10. *The Tacit Dimension,* p. 20.

11. *Personal Knowledge,* p. vii.

12. Two professional associations, the Polanyi Society—in the United States— and the Convivium—in the United Kingdom—have begun this important task.

13. *The Tacit Dimension,* pp. 82-83.

Chapter I

1. Michael Polanyi, "Why Did We Destroy Europe?", *Studium Generale*, 23 (1970), pp. 909-16.

2. Ibid., p. 909.

3. "On the Modern Mind," *Encounter*, 24 (May 1965), p. 12.

4. "Works of Art," chap. 2, p. 30, in "Meaning," unpublished lectures at the University of Texas and the University of Chicago, Feb.-May 1969.

5. Ibid., p. 31.

6. A recurring topic in Polanyi's writings, representative discussions can be found in "Why Did We Destroy Europe?", "Beyond Nihilism," *Knowing and Being*, ed. Marjorie Grene (Chicago: University of Chicago Press, 1969), pp. 3-23, and *Personal Knowledge*, chap. 7.

7. Michael Polanyi, *Personal Knowledge: Towards a Post-Critical Philosophy* (Chicago: University of Chicago Press, 1958), p. 230.

8. Ibid., p. 233.

9. The distinction between the objective ideal of knowledge and genuine objectivity in Polanyi's thought, as pointed out in the Introduction, is essential to understanding this issue. Cf. pp. xvii-xviii.

10. *Personal Knowledge*, p. 132f. and chap. 5.

11. Michael Polanyi, "Scientific Outlook: Its Sickness and Its Cure," *Science*, 125 (March 1957), pp. 480-504.

12. *Knowing and Being*, p. 3.

13. *Personal Knowledge*, p. 227.

14. *Knowing and Being*, p. 8.

15. *Personal Knowledge*, p. 232.

16. Ibid., p. 233.

17. "The Message of the Hungarian Revolution," *Knowing and Being*, pp. 24-39.

18. Jacques Monod, *Chance and Necessity* (London: Collins, 1972), p. 163.

19. "The Two Cultures," *Encounter*, 13 (March 1959), pp. 61-64.

20. Karl Popper's *Objective Knowledge* (Oxford: The Clarendon Press, 1972) is confined mainly to the problem of induction. His solution derives from a belief in the explicitness and exactness thought to exist in the scientific method, an error exposed by Polanyi's evidence for the tacit component of all knowledge.

21. *Personal Knowledge*, pp. 139-42; "Science and Man," *Proceedings of the Royal Society of Medicine*, 62 (September 1970), pp. 969-70.

22. "Science and Man," p. 969.

23. Polanyi's analysis of these problems can be seen in "On Body and Mind," *The New Scholasticism*, 43 (Spring 1969), pp. 195-204, and "Life's Irreducible Structure," *Knowing and Being*, pp. 225-39.

24. *Personal Knowledge*, pp. 6-9.

25. Ibid., p. 269.

26. Ibid.

27. "Science and Man," p. 971f.

28. *Knowing and Being*, p. 7.

29. "Science and Man," p. 972.

30. Ibid.

31. Michael Polanyi, "Genius in Science," *Encounter*, 38 (January 1972), pp. 43-50.

32. Karl Popper, *The Logic of Scientific Discovery* (London: Hutchinson, 1959), p. 16.

33. Michael Polanyi, "The Creative Imagination," *Chemical and Engineering News*, 44 (April 1966), pp. 85-93.

34. *Personal Knowledge*, pp. 9-11.

35. "Genius in Science," p. 46.

36. Ibid.

Chapter II

1. "LeComte du Nouy Foundation Award to Michael Polanyi," *The Christian Scholar*, 43 (March 1960), p. 58.

2. Cf. Melvin Calvin's and Eugene Wigner's contribution to the Michael Polanyi *Festschrift*, *The Logic of Personal Knowledge* (Glencoe, Illinois: The Free Press, 1961).

3. Interview with Magda Polanyi, Oxford, England, December 7, 1973.

4. *The Logic of Personal Knowledge*, p. 12.

5. Cf. "The Potential Theory of Adsorption" in *Knowing and Being*, pp. 87-96, for Polanyi's account of this important episode.

6. Ibid., p. 94.

7. "My Time with X-Rays and Crystals," *Knowing and Being*, pp. 97–104.

8. Ibid., p. 98.

9. Michael Polanyi, *The Tacit Dimension* (Garden City: Doubleday, 1966), p. 3.

10. "U.S.S.R. Economics—Fundamental Data, System and Spirit," *The Manchester School of Economic and Social Studies*, 6 (November 1935), p. 79.

11. Michael Polanyi, *The Logic of Liberty* (Chicago: University of Chicago Press, 1958), p. 170.

13. "The Value of the Inexact," *Philosophy of Science*, 3 (April 1936), pp. 233–34.

13. *Nature*, 140 (October 23, 1937), p. 710.

14. *Nature*, 157 (January 25, 1941), p. 119.

15. "The Struggle between Truth and Propaganda," *The Manchester School of Economic and Social Studies*, 7 (1936), pp. 105–18.

16. "Bibliography of Scientific Papers by Michael Polanyi," *The Logic of Personal Knowledge*, pp. 239–48.

17. Interview, University of California, Berkeley, January 12, 1965.

18. Cf. *Full Employment and Free Trade* (Cambridge: Cambridge University Press, 1945) and *Unemployment and Money*, a diagrammatic film prepared with the assistance of Miss Mary Field, Mr. R. Jeffryes, and Professor J. Jewkes.

19. Professor Kathleen Bliss is currently preparing an account of this group in a book on Joseph Oldham.

20. *The Logic of Liberty*, pp. 3–7.

21. Michael Polanyi, *Science, Faith and Society* (Chicago: University of Chicago Press, 1964).

22. Ibid., p. 32.

23. Michael Polanyi, *Personal Knowledge: Towards a Post-Critical Philosophy* (Chicago: University of Chicago Press, 1958), p. vii–viii. Quoted by permission of University of Chicago Press and Routledge and Kegan Paul, London.

24. Michael Polanyi, *The Study of Man* (Chicago: University of Chicago Press, 1959).

25. Among these major appointments were the Alexander White Professorship at the University of Chicago, the Eddington Lecture at Cambridge

University, the Gunning Lecture at Edinburgh University, Distinguished Visiting Scholar at the University of Virginia, the McInerney Lectures at the University of California, Berkeley, the Terry Lectures at Yale University, and the James B. Duke Visiting Professorship at Duke University. Polanyi was also on the Committee on Social Thought at the University of Chicago, a Fellow at the Center for Advanced Studies in the Behavioral Sciences at Stanford, and a Senior Research Fellow at the Center for Advanced Studies at Wesleyan University.

26. Michael Polanyi and Harry Prosch, *Meaning* (Chicago: University of Chicago Press, 1975).

Chapter III

1. For the importance of the concept of a paradigm, see the second edition of Thomas Kuhn's *The Structure of Scientific Revolutions* (Chicago: University of Chicago Press, 1970).

2. Marie Boas Hall, *Nature and Nature's Laws* (New York: Harper & Row, 1970), p. 1f.

3. Michael Polanyi, *Science, Faith and Society* (Chicago: University of Chicago Press, 1964), p. 22f.

4. Michael Polanyi, "The Creative Imagination," *Chemical and Engineering News*, 44 (April 1966), p. 89.

5. *Knowing and Being*, ed. Marjorie Grene (Chicago: University of Chicago Press, 1969), p. 125.

6. Michael Polanyi, *The Tacit Dimension* (Garden City: Doubleday, 1966), p. 4f.

7. Michael Polanyi, *Personal Knowledge: Towards a Post-Critical Philosophy* (Chicago: University of Chicago Press, 1958), p. 92.

8. Ibid., p. 91.

9. *Economica*, 8 (November 1941), p. 432.

10. *The Tacit Dimension*, p. 6.

11. Ibid.

12. Ibid., pp. 7–10.

13. Michael Polanyi, "Logic and Psychology," *American Psychologist*, 23 (January 1968), p. 30f.

14. *The Tacit Dimension*, p. 19; *Personal Knowledge*, p. 75f.

15. *The Tacit Dimension*, p. 4.

16. Ibid., p. 10; *Personal Knowledge*, p. 55f.; *The Study of Man* (Chicago: University of Chicago Press, 1959), p. 30; *Knowing and Being*, p. 140.

17. *The Tacit Dimension*, p. 10.

18. Ibid. Polanyi calls this aspect the "functional structure of tacit knowing."

19. *Knowing and Being*, pp. 143–44, 201–5.

20. *The Tacit Dimension*, pp. 15–17.

21. Cf. "Appendix," *Intellect and Hope*, eds. Thomas A. Langford and William H. Poteat (Durham: Duke University Press, 1968), pp. 449–55.

22. *The Tacit Dimension*, p. 18.

23. Ibid., p. 13.

24. Ibid.

25. *Personal Knowledge*, pp. 300–53; *The Tacit Dimension*, p. 78; *Knowing and Being*, pp. 133–34.

26. The object of focal awareness may be an idea or problem that we indwell as well as a tangible experience.

27. *Knowing and Being*, p. 105.

28. Wolfe Mays, "Editorial," *Journal of the British Society for Phenomenology*, 4 (October 1973), pp. 199–200.

29. Harry Prosch, "Polanyi's Tacit Knowing in the 'Classic' Philosophers," ibid., pp. 201–15.

30. Ibid., pp. 201–5.

31. Ibid., pp. 205–9.

32. Ibid., pp. 209–15.

33. Ian C. Barbour, *Issues in Science and Religion* (New York: Harper & Row, 1966), p. 138.

34. Arthur Koestler, *The Sleepwalkers* (New York: Grosset & Dunlap, 1959).

35. N. R. Hanson, *Patterns of Discovery* (Cambridge: Cambridge University Press, 1958).

36. Stephen Toulmin, *Foresight and Understanding* (New York: Harper & Row, 1961), and Thomas S. Kuhn, *op. cit.*

37. Irving M. Copi, "Crucial Experiments," *The Structure of Science*, ed. E. H. Madden (Boston: Houghton Mifflin, 1960), and Henry Margenau, *The Nature of Physical Reality* (New York: Harcourt, Brace and World, 1961).

[164]

Chapter IV

1. William Scott, "Polanyi's Theory of Personal Knowledge: A Gestalt Philosophy," *The Massachusetts Review*, 3 (Winter 1962), pp. 349–68.

2. Michael Polanyi, *The Study of Man* (Chicago: University of Chicago Press, 1959), pp. 37–39.

3. Michael Polanyi, *The Tacit Dimension*, (Garden City: Doubleday, 1966), p. 32.

4. Michael Polanyi, *Personal Knowledge: Towards a Post-Critical Philosophy* (Chicago: University of Chicago press, 1958), pp. 381–82.

5. Ibid., pp. 265–68.

6. Michael Polanyi, "Genius in Science," *Encounter*, 38 (January 1972), p. 43; Michael Polanyi, "Science and Reality," *British Journal for the Philosophy of Science*, 18 (November 1967), p. 177.

7. "Genius in Science," p. 44; "The Creative Imagination," *Chemical and Engineering News*, 44 (April 1966), p. 86.

8. "The Creative Imagination," p. 86.

9. "Genius in Science," p. 44.

10. "The Creative Imagination," p. 87.

11. Ibid.

12. *Knowing and Being*, ed. Marjorie Grene (Chicago: University of Chicago Press, 1969), p. 202.

13. "The Creative Imagination," p. 89.

14. Ibid.

15. Ibid.

16. *Knowing and Being*, pp. 53–54.

17. "The Creative Imagination," p. 85.

18. *Personal Knowledge*, pp. 49–65.

19. *The Tacit Dimension*, pp. 15–16.

20. *Personal Knowledge*, pp. 71–77.

21. Ibid., p. 100.

22. Ibid., p. 93.

23. Ibid., p. 363.

24. Ibid.

25. *The Tacit Dimension*, p. 51.

26. *Personal Knowledge*, Part IV, pp. 327–405; *The Tacit Dimension*, chaps. 2 and 3, pp. 27–92.

27. *Personal Knowledge*, p. 3.

28. *The Tacit Dimension*, p. 47.

29. Ibid., p. 35.

30. Ibid.

31. Ibid., p. 36.

32. Ibid., p. 38.

33. Ibid., p. 40.

34. *Personal Knowledge*, p. 330.

35. *Knowing and Being*, pp. 225–39.

36. Ibid., p. 229.

37. Francis Crick, *Of Molecules and Men* (Seattle: University of Washington Press, 1966), pp. 10–16.

38. *The Tacit Dimension*, pp. 46–48.

39. Ibid., p. 46.

40. Jacques Monod, *Chance and Necessity* (London: Collins, 1970).

41. *The Tacit Dimension*, p. 50.

42. Ibid., chap. 3, pp. 55–92.

43. Ibid., p. 80.

44. *Personal Knowledge*, p. 165.

45. *The Tacit Dimension*, pp. xi, 8–81.

46. Ibid., p. 83.

47. Michael Polanyi, *Science, Faith and Society* (Chicago: University of Chicago Press, 1964), pp. 45-46.

48. *The Tacit Dimension*, p. 83.

49. "Meaning," unpublished lecture, University of Chicago, May 1970, pp. 3–8.

50. Ibid. Cf. Harry Prosch, *Cooling the Modern Mind* (Saratoga Springs: Skidmore College, 1971), pp. 20-26, and Bruno V. Manno, "Michael Polanyi on the Problem of Science and Religion," *Zygon*, 9 (March 1974), pp. 51-53.

51. Michael Polanyi and Harry Prosch, *Meaning* (Chicago: University of Chicago Press, 1975), pp. 70-73.

52. Ibid., pp. 70-71.

53. Ibid., p. 72.

54. Ibid., p. 73.

55. Ibid., p. 117.

56. Ibid., p. 75.

57. Ibid., p. 77.

58. Ibid.

59. Ibid., p. 78.

60. "What Is a Painting?", *American Scholar*, 39 (Autumn 1970), pp. 625-69.

61. Ibid., p. 656f.

62. Ibid., p. 664.

63. *Meaning*, p. 88.

64. *Cooling the Modern Mind*, p. 30.

65. Ibid., p. 31; *Personal Knowledge*, pp. 214-24.

66. *Personal Knowledge*, p. 388.

67. Ibid., p. 403.

68. *The Tacit Dimension*, p. 78.

Chapter V

1. Michael Polanyi, *The Tacit Dimension* (Garden City: Doubleday, 1966), p. 83.

2. Besides the Polanyi Society of Explorers and the graduate research at Duke University mentioned in the Introduction, The Study Group on Foundations of Cultural Unity and its successor now known as The Study Group have explored allied themes and issues of Polanyi's thought with some of the most prominent thinkers in the arts and sciences. Out of their conferences have come three books edited by Marjorie Grene, and the last one was dedicated to Polanyi. These books are: *The Anatomy of Knowledge* (Amherst: University of Massachusetts Press, 1969); *Toward a Unity of Knowledge* (New York: International Universities Press, 1969); and *Interpretations of Life and Mind* (New York: Humanities Press, 1971). For evidence of the independent yet convergent trend of thought toward a new paradigm of knowledge, the presentations of these conferences assembled ably by Professor Grene are of major importance.

3. Helmut Kuhn, "Personal Knowledge and the Crisis of the Philosophical Tradition," *Intellect and Hope*, eds. Thomas A. Langford and William H. Poteat (Durham: Duke University Press, 1968), pp. 111–35.

4. Ibid., p. 112.

5. Ibid., pp. 113–14.

6. Ibid., pp. 114–15.

7. Ibid., p. 117.

8. Ibid., p. 120.

9. Ibid.

10. Ibid., p. 121.

11. Ibid., p. 123.

12. Ibid., p. 124.

13. Ibid., p. 132.

14. Ludwig Wittgenstein (New York: Macmillan Co., 1953), p. 6e.

15. Cahal Daly, "Polanyi and Wittgenstein," *Intellect and Hope*, pp. 136–68.

16. Ibid., p. 137.

17. Ibid., p. 138.

18. Ibid., p. 139.

19. Ibid., p. 145.

20. Ibid., p. 141.

21. Ibid., p. 143.

22. Ibid., pp. 149–52.

23. Ibid., p. 146.

24. Ibid., p. 161.

25. Thomas S. Kuhn, *The Structure of Scientific Revolutions* (Chicago: University of Chicago Press, 1970), p. 149 *et passim*.

26. Daly, pp. 154–56.

27. Michael Polanyi, *The Study of Man* (Chicago: University of Chicago Press, 1959), p. 65, quoted by Daly, *op. cit.*, p. 158.

28. Daly, p. 159.

29. Ian Ramsey, "Polanyi and J. L. Austin," *Intellect and Hope*, pp. 169–97.

30. William Poteat, "Myths, Stories, History, Eschatology and Action: Some Polanyian Meditations," *Intellect and Hope*, pp. 198–231.

31. Ibid., p. 204f.

32. Ibid., p. 210.

33. Ibid., p. 231.

34. Daly, p. 168.

35. Marjorie Grene, "Tacit Knowing and the Pre-reflective Cogito," *Intellect and Hope*, pp. 19–57.

36. Ibid., pp. 33–37.

37. Donald Millholand, "Beyond Nihilism: A Study of the Thought of Albert Camus and Michael Polanyi" (Ph.D. Dissertation, Duke University, 1966).

38. *Knowing and Being*, ed. Marjorie Grene (Chicago: University of Chicago Press, 1969), pp. 200, 155–56; Michael Polanyi, *Science, Faith and Society* (Chicago: University of Chicago Press, 1964), p. 12.

39. Daly, pp. 165–66.

40. Ramsey, p. 182.

41. Stephen Toulmin, *Foresight and Understanding* (New York: Harper and Row, 1961).

42. Leonard K. Nash, *The Nature of the Natural Sciences* (Boston: Little, Brown, 1963), p. viif.

43. Ibid., p. 168.

44. Ibid., p. 9.

45. Ibid., pp. 14, 22, 37.

46. Ibid., p. 157.

47. Ibid., p. viii.

48. William T. Scott, "Polanyi's Theory of Personal Knowledge: A Gestalt Philosophy," *The Massachusetts Review*, 3 (Winter 1962), pp. 349–68, and "A Course in Science and Religion Following the Ideas of Michael Polanyi," *The Christian Scholar*, 47 (Spring 1964), pp. 36–46; "A Bridge from Science to Religion Based on Polanyi's Theory of Knowledge," *Zygon*, 5 (March 1970), pp. 41–62.

49. "The Gentle Rain: A Search for Understanding," *Intellect and Hope*, pp. 242–74.

50. Ibid., pp. 244–45.

51. Ibid., p. 246.

52. Ibid., pp. 248-49.

53. Ibid., p. 247.

54. Ibid., pp. 248-53.

55. Ibid., p. 243.

56. W. H. Thorpe, *Animal Nature and Human Nature* (New York: Anchor, 1974), chap. 10; Paul A. Weiss, "The Living System: Determinism Stratified," *Beyond Reductionism*, eds. Arthur Koestler and J. R. Symthies (Boston: Beacon Press, 1971), p. 21 *et passim*.

57. Francis Walshe, "Personal Knowledge and Concepts in the Biological Sciences," *Intellect and Hope*, pp. 275-77.

58. Ibid., p. 276.

59. Ibid., p. 281-84.

60. Ibid., pp. 290-93.

61. Ibid., p. 296.

62. Ibid., p. 299.

63. Ibid., p. 302.

64. Ibid., p. 303.

65. Ibid., pp. 305-7.

66. Ibid., p. 311.

67. Arthur Peacocke, *Science and the Christian Experiment* (London: Oxford University Press, 1971), pp. 10, 15, 85f.

68. Ibid., p. 85.

69. Ibid., p. 86.

70. Abraham H. Maslow, *The Psychology of Science* (New York: Harper & Row, 1966), pp. xvi-xvii; Carl Rogers, "Some New Challenges," *The American Psychologist*, 28 (May 1973), p. 379.

71. Maslow, p. 18.

72. Carl Rogers, "On Our Science of Man," *Man and the Science of Man*, eds. William R. Coulson and Carl R. Rogers (Columbus: Charles E. Merrill, 1968), pp. 55-72.

73. Ibid., p. 59.

74. Ibid., p. 8.

75. Ibid., pp. 70-71.

76. Robert N. Bellah, *Beyond Belief* (New York: Harper & Row, 1970), pp. 252-53.

77. Raymond Aron, "Max Weber and Michael Polanyi," *Intellect and Hope*, p. 341.

78. Ibid., p. 363.

79. Ibid., pp. 347-60.

80. Bertrand de Jouvenel, "The Republic of Science," *The Logic of Personal Knowledge* (Glencoe, Illinois: Free Press, 1961), p. 131.

81. Ibid., pp. 140-41.

82. Carl Friedrich, "Man the Measure: Personal Knowledge and the Quest for Natural Law," *Intellect and Hope*, pp. 91-110.

83. Ibid., p. 91.

84. *Scientific Change*, ed. A. Crombie (New York: Basic Books, 1963), p. 392.

85. Ibid., p. 379f.

86. M. H. Pirenne, *Optics, Painting and Photography* (Cambridge: Cambridge University Press, 1970), with a Foreword by Michael Polanyi.

87. Ibid., p. 11.

88. Ibid., p. 183.

89. Ibid.

90. *Supra*, chapter IV.

91. Arthur Koestler, *The Act of Creation* (New York: Dell, 1967); Donald L. Weismann, "In Pursuit of Discovery," *Intellect and Hope*, pp. 386-401.

92. *The Tacit Dimension*, p. 80.

93. "In Pursuit of Discovery," p. 387.

94. Ibid., p. 401.

95. Ibid.

96. Richard Gelwick, "Discovery and Theology," *Scottish Journal of Theology*, 28 (August 1975), pp 301-22.

97. Michael Polanyi, "Science and Religion: Separate Dimensions or Common Ground?" *Philosophy Today*, 7 (Spring 1963), pp. 4-14.

98. H. Richard Niebuhr, *Radical Monotheism and Western Culture* (New York: Harper and Brothers, 1960), p. 131.

99. Malcolm Jeeves, *The Scientific Enterprise and Christian Faith* (London: Tyndale Press, 1969), pp. 31-44.

100. Thomas Langford, "Michael Polanyi and the Task of Theology," *Journal of Religion*, 46 (January 1966), pp. 45-55.

101. For development of Polanyi's general implications for Christian theology see Gelwick, *Credere Aude* (Ann Arbor: University Microfilms, 1965), chaps. I, VII, and VIII.

102. Jerry Gill, *The Possibility of Religious Knowledge* (Grand Rapids: William B. Eerdmans, 1971), p. 7.

103. Ibid., p. 117.

104. Thomas F. Torrance, *Theological Science* (London: Oxford University Press, 1969).

105. Thomas F. Torrance, "The Integration of Form in Natural and in Theological Science," *Science, Medicine and Man*, vol. 1 (Elmsford, New York: Pergamon Press, 1973), pp. 143-72.

106. Ibid., p. 168.

107. Ibid.

108. Bernard J. F. Lonergan, *Insight: A Study of Human Understanding* (London: Longmans, Green, 1958)

109. Ibid., p. ix; Polanyi, *Science, Faith and Society*, pp. 8-9.

110. Lonergan, p. ix.

111. Langdon Gilkey, *Religion and the Scientific Future* (New York: Harper & Row, 1970), pp. 42-43 *et passim*.

112. Harold Schilling, *The New Consciousness in Science and Religion* (Philadelphia: Pilgrim Press, 1973).

Chapter VI

1. This title is used in a slightly different yet related form in Polanyi's article in *The Virginia Quarterly Review*, 38 (Spring 1962), pp. 177-95.

2. Cf. Chapter I.

3. Cf. Alvin Toffler, *Future Shock* (New York: Bantam Books, 1972).

4. Robert L. Heilbroner, "The Human Prospect," *The New York Review of Books*, 20 (January 24, 1974), pp. 21-34.

5. Cf. Gerald LaFayette Smith, "Tacit Knowing and the Logic of Tradition: A Study in the Thought of Michael Polanyi" (Ph.D. dissertation, Duke University, 1970).

6. Marjorie Grene's book *The Knower and the Known* (New York: Basic Books, 1966) is especially helpful in treating this issue historically and in relation to Polanyi's epistemology.

7. *The Knower and the Known*, p. 17.

8. Ibid., pp. 41–43.

9. Ibid., pp. 67, 73–79.

10. Ibid., p. 102.

11. Ibid., p. 120.

12. Ibid., p. 143.

13. Erwin Schrödinger, *Mind and Matter* (London: Cambridge University Press, 1958), pp. 38f, 43, 66.

14. Grene, "Tacit Knowing and the Pre-reflective Cogito," *Intellect and Hope*, eds. Thomas A. Langford and William H. Poteat (Durham: Duke University Press, 1968), p. 32.

15. Michael Polanyi, *The Tacit Dimension* (Garden City: Doubleday, 1966), pp. xi, 85.

16. *The Knower and the Known*, p. 158.

17. Michael Polanyi, *Personal Knowledge: Towards a Post-Critical Philosophy* (Chicago: University of Chicago Press, 1958), pp. 27–30, 253–61.

18. *The Knower and the Known*, p. 179.

19. José Delgado's book *Physical Control of the Mind* (New York: Harper & Row, 1969), while granting more to the status of mind than the others listed here, fails, however, to see what Polanyi has achieved in his principle of dual control and thinks of control only at the level of the boundary conditions.

20. Cf. *Beyond Reductionism* and *Interpretations of Life and Mind* referred to in Chapter V.

21. *The Knower and the Known*, p. 195.

22. *The Tacit Dimension*, chap. II.

23. "On the Modern Mind," *Encounter*, 24 (May 1965), p. 14.

24. "On Body and Mind," *The New Scholasticism*, 43 (Spring 1969), pp. 195–204.

25. Cf. Chapter V.

26. *Toward a Unity of Knowledge*, ed. Marjorie Grene (New York: International Universities Press, 1969), p. 200.

27. Professor Edward Pols in "Polanyi and the Problem of Metaphysical Knowledge," *Intellect and Hope*, p. 82, makes the keen observation that Polanyi agrees with Hume on our participation in our knowledge yet instead of concluding with skepticism, Polanyi concludes with the notion that our participation is what makes it knowledge.

28. *Personal Knowledge*, p. 324.

29. *The Tacit Dimension*, p. 92.

30. Marjorie Grene, "Hobbes and the Modern Mind," *The Anatomy of Knowledge*, ed. Marjorie Grene (Amherst: University of Massachusetts Press, 1969), p. 4.

31. "The Message of the Hungarian Revolution," *Knowing and Being*, ed. Marjorie Grene (Chicago: University of Chicago Press, 1969), pp. 24–39.

32. Cf. Chapter I.

33. "Message of the Hungarian Revolution," pp. 27–28.

34. Ibid., p. 26.

35. Ibid., p. 28f.

36. Ibid., p. 29.

37. Schilling, *The New Consciousness in Science and Religion* (Philadelphia: Pilgrim Press, 1973), pp. 129–30.

38. These lines were received by him in the Fall of 1962 when Polanyi was a Fellow at the Institute for Advanced Studies in Behavioral Sciences, Stanford, California.

BIBLIOGRAPHY

For further investigation of the range of Michael Polanyi's thought, two extensive bibliographies are already published as follows:

Gelwick, Richard L. "A Bibliography of Michael Polanyi's Social and Philosophical Writings," *Intellect and Hope: Essays in the Thought of Michael Polanyi,* eds. Thomas A. Langford and William H. Poteat. Durham: Duke University Press, 1968, pp. 432-46. This bibliography contains a list of Polanyi's books and brochures, articles appearing in books, and articles published in journals from 1935 to 1967. In addition, there is a list of critical reviews of Polanyi's thought.

Polanyi, John. "Scientific Papers by Michael Polanyi," *The Logic of Personal Knowledge: Essays Presented to Michael Polanyi on His Seventieth Birthday.* Glencoe, Illinois: The Free Press, 1961, pp. 239-48. The list covers from 1910 to 1949 and numbers 218 scientific papers. A brief list of Polanyi's other publications is also given.

In addition to the above bibliographical resources and the works cited in this book the following publications of Michael Polanyi should be mentioned.

"The Body-Mind Relation," with discussion by Polanyi and Yehoshua Bar-Hillel, *Man and the Science of Man,* eds. William R. Coulson and Carl R. Rogers. Columbus, Ohio: Charles E. Merrill Publishing Co., 1968, pp. 85-130.

"A Conversation with Michael Polanyi," Interviewer Mary Harrington Hall, *Psychology Today,* 1 (May 1968), pp. 20-25, 65-67.

"The Determinants of Social Action," *Roads to Freedom: Essays in Honor of Friederich von Hayek,* ed. Erich Streissler. New York: Augustus M. Kelley Publishers, 1969, pp. 165-79.

[175]

BIBLIOGRAPHY

"A Dialogue: Michael Polanyi and Carl R. Rogers," *Man and the Science of Man*, pp. 193–201.

"Do Life Processes Transcend Physics and Chemistry?" Symposium with Gerald Holton, Ernest Nagel, John R. Platt, and Barry Commoner, *Zygon*, 3 (December 1968), pp. 442–72.

Scientific Thought and Social Reality, Fred Schwartz (ed.), New York: International Universities Press, 1974.

"Transcendence and Self-Transcendence," *Soundings*, 3 (Spring 1970) pp. 88–94.

Index

Aberdeen, University of, 47
Absurdist world view, 3, 13, 24, 147, 150
Analytical philosophy, 51, 115-18
Archimedes, 70
Aristotle, 78, 79, 114, 142-43
Aron, Raymond, 126
Art, 105, 129-32
Augustinian principle, 132
Austin, John, 115, 117, 133
Awareness. See Focal awareness; Subsidiary awareness; Tacit knowing

Bacon, Francis, 80
Baillie, John, 41
Barbour, Ian C., 164
Bar-Hillel, Yehoshua, 175
Behaviorism, 116-17
Belief and knowledge, 157
Bellah, Robert, 126
Bentham, Jeremy, 20
Bernal, J. D., 38
Bliss, Kathleen, 41, 162
Boundary conditions, 97, 147
British Association for the Advancement of Science, 41
Brodbeck, May, 159
Budapest, 30, 31
Bukharin, N. I., 35

Calling, acceptance of, 111-12, 157-58
Calvin, Melvin, 41, 61
Camus, Albert, 118-19, 159

Carson, Rachel, 71
Cartesian dualism, 118, 144
Chance and necessity, 98
Classic philosophy, 78-79
Cloud physics, 121-22
Commoner, Barry, 176
Computers, 148
Condorcet, M. J. A. N., 19
Congrès du Palais de la Découverte, international scientific meeting in 1937, 37-38
Congress for Cultural Freedom, 53
Consciousness, 147-48
Convivium, 159
Copernicus, 17, 25, 44, 56, 57, 86
Copi, Irving M., 81
Coulson, William, 125
Crick, Francis, 146
Crisis of belief, xiii; a religious issue, xiv
Crisis of culture, xii-xiv, 3-4, 137-38, 149; in historical perspective, 4-24

Dalton, John, 44
Daly, Cahal, 115-16
Darwin, Charles, 44, 147
Davies, P. M. C., 159
Deductive process, 80
Delgado, José, 146, 173
Democritus, 16
Descartes, René, 18, 47, 142-43
Destructiveness of twentieth century, xviii, 4

Dichotomies, an end to, 70, 141–49
Diderot, Denis, 19
Discovery in science: basis for true objectivity, xiii; bearing on reality, 85–91; choice of problem, 25, 88; imagination and intuition, 88–90; key concept, xi–xii, 26, 85; kinship with art, 43, 130, 139–40; logic of evolution and, 155–56; nature of, 24–28, 85–94, 99–100; origin of, 25; role of community in, 36, 39–40, 44–45, 80; role of tradition in, 36, 44–45, 76; skill, 121; unformalizable components in, 42–44; verification, proof, testing, 80, 90
Distal term, 67
DNA, 97, 124
Donne, John, 3
Dostoevsky, Fyodor, xiii, 22
Doubt: growth of, 18; in fiduciary framework, 151; modern skepticism, 18, 20, 22; of tradition, 8
Dual control, 96, 98
Durham, University of, 42
Dynamo-objective coupling, 7–8, 10–13

Ehrlich, Paul, 74
Einstein, Albert, 25, 27, 32, 44, 87, 134, 152
Eliot, T. S., 41
Engels, Friedrich, 22
Enlightenment, 19, 20
Eriksen, C. W., 63
Error, 91, 98, 112
Evolution, theory of, 94–99
Existential belief, 100
Existentialism, 118–20, 145
Experiment and interpretation, 80

Fact and value separation, 145–47
Factual statements, 146
Falsifiability, 90–91
Fiduciary character of knowing, 49, 151
Field, Mary, 162
Focal awareness, 49, 63, 67. See also Tacit knowing
Freedom of science, 35–41, 61, 100
French Revolution, 11, 19
Friedrich, Carl, 127

Galileo, 16, 142

Galileo Circle, 31
Gelwick, Richard, 171, 172, 175
German Romantic nihilism, 12
Gestalt philosophy, 83
Gestalt psychology, 26, 43, 48, 61–62
Gifford Lectures, 47, 112
Gilkey, Langdon, 135
Gill, Jerry, 133–34
Gimes, Miklos, 154
Greek Pyrrhonism, 16
Greek thought, 141
Grene, Marjorie, 118, 142, 147, 160, 167, 172

Haber, Fritz, 32–34
Hall, Mary Boas, 163
Hall, Mary Harrington, 175
Hanson, N. R., 80
Hayek, Friedrich von, 175
Hazard inherent in knowing, 51, 76, 77, 93
Hegel, Georg W. F., 22, 113
Heilbroner, Robert L., 172
Herzog, Reginald Oliver, 34
Heuristic field, 108
Heuristic philosophy: defined, 84; appropriateness to Polanyi, xv–xvi, 84–85; bearing on fields of study, 101–7
Historicism, 10, 113, 114
Hobbes, Thomas, 20
Hodges, H. A., 41
Hogben, Lancelot Thomas, 38
Holton, Gerald, 28
Hope and scientific understanding, xiv, 150–51
Human person: eclipsed by scientific method, 17–18; evolutionary perspective, 155–56; as explorer, 8, 108, 111; intelligence, 91; knowing, 51; study of, 125, 147–48; time perspective, 156
Humanistic psychology, 125–26
Humanity, meaning of, 157
Hume, David, 18, 21, 78, 79, 80, 143–44
Hungarian Revolution of 1956, 13, 152–55
Husserl, Edmund, 88

Ideals, traditional and transcendent, xiii, 12–13, 155–56
Ignotus, Paul, 31

Imagination, 88-90
Inductive method, 80
Indwelling, 70, 98, 139. *See also* Tacit knowing
Intelligence: evolution of, 8-9, 91; mechanical, 148
Intuition, 88-90
Inverted spectacles, 87, 88-89

Jeeves, Malcolm, 171
Jeffryes, R., 162
Jewkes, J., 162
Jouvenel, Bertrand de, 127

Kaiser Wilhelm Institute for Fiber Chemistry, 34
Kaiser Wilhelm Institute for Physical Chemistry, 32
Kant, Immanuel, 18, 78, 143-44
Kepler, Johannes, 17
Koestler, Arthur, 130-31
Kuethe, J. L., 63
Köhler, Wolfgang, 61
Kuhn, Helmut, 113-15
Kuhn, Thomas S., 5, 80, 116, 128-29

Langford, Thomas, 133, 159
Laplacean ideal, 15, 96, 122, 147
Lazarus, K. S., 62
LeComte du Noüy Foundation Award, 29
Leibniz, G. W. von, 88
Lenin, V. I., 36
Levy-Brühl, Lucien, 10
Life: evolution of, 94-99; knowing, 51, 94, 144; levels of, 91-92, 94-99. *See also* Boundary conditions; Dual control; Marginal control; Modern biology; Operational principles; Sentience
Locke, John, 16, 21
Logical positivism, 145
Lonergan, J. F. Bernard, 135-36

McCleary, R. A., 7
McKinley, G. M., 156
MacKinnon, D. M., 41
Mach, Ernst, 21

Malinowski, Bronislaw, 159
Manchester, University of, 35, 42
Mannheim, Karl, 41
Manno, Bruno V., 166
Margenau, Henry, 81
Marginal control, 96, 122, 147
Marx, Karl, 22
Marxism, 11, 22
Maslow, Abraham, 125, 148
Mathematics, 17
Mays, Wolfe, 164
Meaning: in art, 105-6; in morality and religion, 106-7; in science, 101; "self-centered," 101-2, 107; "self-giving," 101-7; tacit integration of clues into, 60-61
Mechanism, 16, 21, 122-23, 140, 146-48
Medical Section of the British Psychological Society, 5
Metaphor, 104-5, 130
Mill, J. S., 80
Millholand, Donald, 118-19
Moberly, Walter, 41
Modern biology, 96-98, 122-24, 147
Modern mind, 5, 7
Monod, Jacques, 14, 146
"The Moot," 41
Moral inversion. *See* Dynamo-objective coupling
Moral perfectionism, 16, 19, 149
Moral skepticism, 16

Nagel, Ernest, 176
Nash, Leonard K., 120-21
Natural law, 127-28
Nature, 37, 39
Nature as our home, 157
Nazi regime, 7, 12
Neumann, John von, 35
Neurobiology, 122
Neurophysiology, 122
Newton, Isaac, 17, 23, 25, 44, 56, 57, 87
Niebuhr, H. Richard, 132-33
Nietzsche, Friedrich, 22
Nihilism, 21-22

Objective ideal: definition, xvii-xviii, 18, 23-24; destructive effects, xvii, 8-10, 13, 15-16, 23, 24, 25, 46, 98-99, 137-38, 156-57; distinguished from

INDEX

objectivity, xvii–xviii; fused with moral passion in dynamo-objective coupling, 7–8, 149–50; relation to positivism, xviii Objective ideal, contradicted. *See Discovery in science; Life, Knowing; Selfset standards; Tacit knowing; Universal intent*
Objectivism. *See Objective ideal*
Objectivity, genuine, xvii, 48
Oldham, Joseph, 41, 162
Ontological aspect, 74. *See also Tacit knowing*
Operational principles, 95, 97
Oxford University, Merton College of, 51

Painting, 105, 129–30
Paradigm, a new: classic philosophical antecedents, 78–79; definition, 55; Polanyi's contribution to, 56–57, 82, 94, 149
Paradigm, signs of change: currently, xv; general public, 81–82; human potential movement, 82; philosophy of science, 79–81
Pauline scheme of redemption, 151
Peacocke, Arthur, 123–24
Perception, 86–88
Perrin, Jean, 38
Personal knowledge: definition of, 48–49; in an evolutionary perspective, 98; in tacit knowing, 93
Petöfi Circle, 153
Phenomenal structure of knowing, 71. *See also Tacit knowing*
Phenomenology, 117, 119
Pipes, Richard, 153
Pirenne, M. H., 129–30
Plato, 56, 78–79, 114, 142–43
Platt, John R., 176
Plays, 105–6
Polanyi, John, 175
Polanyi, Magda, 161
Polanyi, Michael: birth, 4; controversiality of, xvi; death, 52; first scientific paper, 32; freedom of science struggle, 35–41; inaugural philosophical address, 42–47; interdisciplinary character of, xvi–xvii, 29–30, 31, 41; later philosophical investigations,

51–52; magnum opus, 47–51; move to England, 35; originality of, xviii, 82; potential theory of adsorption episode, 32–34; professional careers from medicine to philosophy, 31–42; selected major appointments, 162–63; success in science, 34–35, 40–41; university education, 30–32
Polanyi Society, The, 159
Political science, 126–28, 154–55
Pols, Edward, 173
Polycentric tasks, 36
Popper, Karl, 160, 161
Positivism, xviii, 21, 115–16, 118; logical, 145
Post-critical philosophy: definition of, 47–48, 56; name for Polanyi's philosophy, 83
Poteat, William, 117, 159
Pound, Ezra, 104
Pragmatism, 119
Prosch, Harry, 52, 106
Proximal term, 67. *See also Tacit knowing*
Psychology and epistemology, 71
Ptolemaic system, 86
Pythagorean tradition, 17

Ramsey, Ian, 117, 119
Reality: definition of, 49, 85; in science, 85, 101; structure of knowing and, 51, 94, 98, 155–56; tacit knowing of, 74, 89; unspecifiable and unrealizable dimensions of, 108
Reductionism, 146–48
Reformation, 18
Religions of the world, xiv
Renaissance, 18
Riddell Lectures, 42
Rituals, 103–4
Rogers, Carl, 125, 148
Romantic individualism, 21
Rousseau, Jean-Jacques, 20, 21
Russell, Bertrand, 33–34
Russian Communist Revolution, 7

Sartre, Jean Paul, 118, 145
Schilling, Harold, 136
Schrödinger, Erwin, 144

[180]

Schwartz, Fred, 176
Science: ambiguity in, 36; at one with human hopes, 139–41; authority in, 33; consequences of mistaken view of, xiv, 6–7, 15, 24; tacit components in, 42–44, 47–51, 52, 100; validity in, 44, 90; value of, xiv, 6; upheld by premises of a free society, 46
Scientific outlook. See Objective ideal
Scientific revolution, 17, 23
Scott, William T., 83, 121–22
"Self-centered" knowing, 101–2, 107
"Self-giving" knowing, 101–7
Self-set standards, 92, 156
Semantic aspect, 74. See also Tacit knowing
Sentience, 98
Shakespeare, William, 104
Skinner, B. F., 146
Smith, Gerald LaFayette, 172
Smythies, J. R., 170
Snow, C. P., 14
Society: calling of, 100; conditions for freedom and pursuit of truth, 8, 108–9
Society for the Freedom of Science, 38
Society of Explorers, image of our calling, xi, 50, 84, 99, 101, 109, 111, 140, 157
Sociology, 126–27
Socrates, 114
Solipsism, 114, 116–17
Soviet economic system, 36
Speech, 96
Spinoza, Benedict, 88
Stalin, Joseph, 153
Stalinist regime, 7, 11
Stratton, G. M., 87
Study Group on the Foundations of Cultural Unity, 167
Subception, 62–63
Subjective, 92
Subsidiary awareness, 49, 63, 67, 70. See also Tacit knowing
Symbols, reality of, 103
Szilard, Leo, 35

Tacit dimension. See Tacit knowing
Tacit knowing: a dimension in fundamental cases of knowing, 57–61, 65–67; "attending to," 67; contradicts objective ideal, 64; diagram of, 76–77;

distal term, 67; functional structure of, 70; Gestalt psychology clue to, 61–62; imagination and intuition, 88–90; indwelling, 70, 98; integration of clues into meaning, 60–61; integration of two forms of knowledge, 63, 86; irreversible achievements, 65; name for Polanyi's philosophy, 83; ontological aspect, 76, 77; phenomenal structure of, 71, 77; philosophy of science and, 79–81; proximal term, 67; "relying on, " 67; role of institutions and tradition in, 106–7; "self-centered" structure, 101–2; "self-giving" structure, 101–7; semantic aspect, 74, 77; structure of all knowing, 63–64, 140; subception, 62–63; technical and theoretical elaboration of terminology, 65–78
Technology, not the basic problem, xiv, 5–6, 137–38
Theology, 132–36
Thorpe, W. H., 170
Toffler, Alvin, 172
Torrance, Thomas F., 134–35
Toulmin, Stephen, 80
Tradition, 76, 93, 116, 139, 155–56
Traditional philosophy, 112–15
Triad of knowing, 63–64
Truth, pursuit of, 100, 114, 152–54
Turgenev, Ivan, 21–22
Twentieth Party Congress, 153

Universal intent, 51, 76, 77, 92, 111, 156

"Value of the Inexact, The," 36–37
Vidler, A. R., 41
Vitalism, 140
Voltaire, 19

Walshe, Francis, 122–23
Ward, Barbara, 74
Weber, Max, 126
Weismann, Donald L., 130–31
Weiss, Paul A., 170
Wigner, Eugene, 35, 149, 161
Wisdom, John, 115, 117–18, 133
Wittgenstein, Ludwig, 115–17, 133